松鼠纳特金和小猪鲁滨逊

比得兔的世界·The World of Peter Rabbit ™

⑤

Squirrel Nutkin and Little Pig Robinson

松鼠纳特金和
小猪鲁滨逊

BEATRIX POTTER

[英] 比阿特丽克斯·波特 著

吴青 陈恕 译

中国少年儿童出版社

图书在版编目(CIP)数据

松鼠纳特金和小猪鲁滨逊／（英）波特著；吴青，陈恕译．－北京：中国少年儿童出版社，2004.4
（比得兔的世界）
ISBN 7-5007-7000-6

Ⅰ.松... Ⅱ.①波...②吴...③陈... Ⅲ.童话-英国-现代 Ⅳ.I561.88

中国版本图书馆CIP数据核字（2004）第028353号

著作权合同登记 图字：01-2004-2228

THE TALE OF SQUIRREL NUTKIN
New reproductions copyright © Frederick Warne & Co., 2002
Original copyright in text and illustrations © Frederick Warne & Co., 1903

THE TALE OF LITTLE PIG ROBINSON
New reproductions copyright © Frederick Warne & Co., 2002
Original copyright in text and illustrations © Frederick Warne & Co., 1930

Frederick Warne & Co. is the owner of all rights,
copyrights and trademarks in the Beatrix Potter character names and illustrations.
Produced under licence from Frederick Warne & Co. Ltd
First published in Great Britain by Frederick Warne & Co. Ltd

本书中英双语版由英国费德里克·沃恩公司(Frederick Warne & Co.)
授权中国少年儿童出版社独家出版

比阿特丽克斯·波特的照片为维克多利亚＆阿尔波特博物馆和沃恩公司资料，并授权使用。

SONG SHU NA TE JIN HE XIAO ZHU LU BIN XUN

出版发行：中国少年儿童新闻出版总社
中国少年儿童出版社

出 版 人：海 飞
执行出版人：赵恒峰

作　　者：比阿特丽克斯·波特（英）	美术编辑：沈苑苑　齐欣
责任编辑：李 华　钱翠霞	责任印务：李书森
社　　址：北京市东四二条21号	邮政编码：100708
总编室：+86-10-64035735	传　　真：+86-10-64012262
h t t p：//www.ccppg.com.cn	E - mail：zbs@ccppg.com.cn
24小时销售咨询服务热线：+86-10-84037667	
印　　刷：山东新华印刷厂德州厂	经　　销：新华书店
开　　本：787×1230　1/32	印　张：5.5
2004年4月山东第1版	2004年4月山东第1次印刷
字　　数：110千字	印　　数：1-20,000
ISBN 7-5007-7000-6/I·537	定　价：20.00元

图书若有印装问题，请随时向印务部退换。

前　言

在世界儿童文学长廊里，活跃着一只最古老而又最年轻，最顽皮而又最惹人喜爱的兔子——比得兔。自从1902年他以在菜园里狼狈逃窜、丢掉了蓝上衣的形象在图画书中登台亮相，他和他的伙伴们便一个接一个地以不可抗拒的魔力闯进了数以千万计孩子的童年生活。

"比得兔"故事系列的诞生本身就是一个童话

比阿特丽克斯·波特（Beatrix Potter, 1866-1943）出生在英国伦敦一个贵族的家庭里，由保姆带大。平日很少与父母见面，也没有玩伴。她的大部分时间是在自家的教室里和家庭女教师、弟弟（11岁以后进入了寄宿学校）一起度过的。小波特和弟弟虽然有时会感到寂寞，但并不无聊。他们在教室里饲养了很多宠物，有兔子、老鼠、鸟、蝙蝠、青蛙、蜥蜴、水龟……波特经常为她的宠物们想像出许多故事来，它们便是"比得兔"故事系列中各种角色的故事原型。波特还以她特有的艺术敏感，把宠物作为模特孜孜不倦地练习绘画，这为她以后的绘画创作打下了坚实的基础。

波特16岁的时候与父亲到英格兰湖区度假，立即就喜欢上了那里的乡村景色。青山秀水给了波特很多灵感，并就此成为比得兔和他的朋友们展开趣味故事的背景。

波特在很小的时候就展露了惊人的绘画天赋，并一直乐此不疲，直至晚年。波特非常喜爱孩子，富于童心童趣，常常用自编自绘的童话给朋友的孩子写信。1893年，波特在给一个患重病的小男孩诺维尔的信里讲述了比得兔的故事："亲爱的诺维尔，我不知道应该给你写些什么，那么就让我给你讲一个关于四只小兔子的故事吧,他们的名字叫做 —— 弗洛普西,默普西,棉球尾还有比得。"1900年,她从诺维尔那里把所有的信件都借回来,进行整理编辑。1902年10月,经过一番波折之后,沃恩公司接受了《比得兔的故事》,印刷了8,000本图文并茂的童话书。书很畅销,到了圣诞节,他们又迅速加印了20,000本。"比得兔"获得了令人意想不到的成功!从此,波特的创作一发不可收,她又陆续出版了《松鼠纳特金的故事》、《格鲁塞斯特的裁缝》、《小兔本杰明的故事》等。如今,"比得兔"故事系列历经百年而魅力不减,行遍世界而神采依然,成为照亮亿万儿童心灵的不朽经典。比阿特丽克斯·波特也因此名垂史册,在世界儿童文学经典作家的长廊里占据了一席重要的不可替代的位置。

"比得兔"故事系列的创作展现了作者超凡脱俗的人格魅力

"比得兔"故事系列不仅为波特赢得了世界性的声誉,而且还为她带来了可观的财富。从1905年开始直至1943年波特去世,她先后在英格兰湖区等地买下了15个农场的约4000英亩的土地,过着与大自然相伴的田园生活。表面上看来,波特的一生浪漫而完美,令人艳羡,而事实却远非如此。她的青少年时期孤独而压抑,比得兔的出版屡受挫折,婚姻生活几经磨难。为了追求独立、自由、幸福、并有所作为,波特不得不时常与生活和命运进行抗争,也正是这些磨难和抗争使波特的人格魅力闪耀出夺人的光彩!

在波特生活的时代,女性社会地位卑微,很少有机会到社会上工作。不甘平庸的波特向命运抗争,向世俗挑战,不断地进行各种社会化的尝试。为了出版《比得兔的故事》,她曾先后向六家出版社投稿,但六次均遭到拒绝。在向沃恩公司做第二次努力时她终于成功了。

波特具有敏锐的超乎常人的商业意识,她积极参与"比得兔"故事系列的一切出版工作,不仅将图书进行准确的定位,而且及时地为比得兔的形象注册了商标,并积极致力于外延产品的开发。她设计的比得兔棋盘游戏还一度成为当时的热销玩具。

婚后,波特曾一度搁笔。1914年,第一次世界大战爆发,沃恩公司陷入财务危机,沃恩家族的管理者被控入狱。作为沃恩家族忠诚的朋友,波特倾全力帮助他们,并重操旧业,以出版《阿普利·达普利的童谣》、《塞西莉·帕斯利的童谣》的利润挽救了沃恩公司。

在后半生,波特以其无私、高尚的品格从事着各种社会公益事业。她经常资助青年女子协会、伤残儿童救助协会和国家信托组织等具有社会公益性质的团体。此外,她几乎把自己全部的财力和后半生的精力都奉献给保护大自然和土地免遭破坏的事业上了。在去世前,她把自己拥有的4000多英亩的土地全部留给了国家信托组织。由于波特的无私奉献,英格兰湖区才得以完好地保存下来,并且那里的人们现在依然按照原有的、传承了几个世纪的农耕形式生活着。

波特高尚的人格和她的艺术成就一样,散发着经久不衰的魅力。她的美丽、富有、无私、高尚,她的坎坷、抗争、独立、奉献,使她的一生成为后人缅怀追思的永远的传奇。

"比得兔"故事系列是童话中的经典杰作

自从1902年首次出版以来,比得兔故事便赢得了全世界孩子们的心,更拥有了过亿的欣赏者,至今已被翻译成36种语言在世界数十个国家出版发行,销售量已逾千万册。在英语国家中,几乎每个孩子手中都会有一两本比得兔的故事,因此它更享有"儿童文学中的圣经"的美誉。"比得兔"故事系列是友情和爱心的颂歌。23篇精美的童话各具异趣,但字里行间都流溢着友情和爱心的温馨。丛书中,爱的美德常常与智慧和力量相伴。在《格鲁塞斯特的裁缝》一书中,当裁缝在缝制衣服遇到困难时,那些平时受他关爱的小老鼠们,用集体的智慧和力量帮他渡过难关。丛书也是抑恶扬善的寓言。在《凶猛坏兔子的故事》中,作者对坏兔子不留情面,让他在失掉胡子和尾巴的痛苦中反省。而对于顽皮兔子比得的惩罚,则完全是一种善意而适度的劝诫。丛书还是文图巧妙结合的优美画卷。一幅幅精美的绘图逐页插配,相映成趣,使诗文美与艺术美融汇成具有哲思意味的梦一般的意境,给人以极大的艺术享受。

  比得兔不仅在文学界久负盛名,而且还逐渐成为芭蕾舞、音乐剧、电影、动画片等其他艺术领域的主角;以比得兔形象为标志的外延产品已经发展成一个世界知名的儿童品牌;以"比得兔"命名的网站正以四种语言运行着,每个月要接待200多万访问者。如今,每年都有75,000多位波特迷到波特住过的山顶农场去追寻她的足迹,感受她从大自然中汲取的创作灵感,更有无数的崇拜者以能收藏波特的任何物品而感到自豪。

  真、善、美是没有国界的。我相信比得兔必将会在中国大地上续写他新的传奇!

目　录

松鼠纳特金的故事　　　　　　　　　　　　　13
The Tale of Squirrel Nutkin

小猪鲁滨逊的故事　　　　　　　　　　　　　51
The Tale of Little Pig Robinson

松鼠纳特金的故事

The Tale of Squirrel Nutkin

1903

这是一个关于"一条尾巴"的故事——一条小红松鼠的尾巴,松鼠的名字叫纳特金。

纳特金有一个哥哥叫闪酱果,他还有许多表兄妹,他们都住在湖边的一片树林里。

This is a tale about a tail — a tail that belonged to a little red squirrel, and his name was Nutkin.

He had a brother called Twinkleberry, and a great many cousins; they lived in a wood at the edge of a lake.

湖心有一座小岛,岛上长满了树木和坚果灌木。其中有一棵空心的橡树,它是一只猫头鹰的家,猫头鹰叫老布朗。

In the middle of the lake there is an island covered with trees and nut bushes; and amongst those trees stands a hollow oak-tree, which is the house of an owl who is called Old Brown.

秋天,当坚果成熟、榛子灌木的叶子变成了金黄色的时候,纳特金、闪酱果,还有其他的小松鼠一起走出树林,到湖边去了。

One autumn when the nuts were ripe, and the leaves on the hazel bushes were golden and green — Nutkin and Twinkleberry and all the other little squirrels came out of the wood, and down to the edge of the lake.

小松鼠们用细树枝捆扎起小木筏,从水上划向猫头鹰岛去采摘坚果。

每只松鼠都带了一个麻袋和一支大桨,他们还把各自的尾巴张开当做风帆。

They made little rafts out of twigs, and they paddled away over the water to Owl Island to gather nuts.

Each squirrel had a little sack and a large oar, and spread out his tail for a sail.

小松鼠们带了三只肥胖的老鼠作为献给老布朗的礼物,他们把老鼠摆在老布朗家的门槛上。

然后,闪酱果和其他小松鼠,向老布朗深深地鞠了一躬,很有礼貌地说:"老布朗先生,您能允许我们在您的岛上摘些坚果吗?"

They also took with them an offering of three fat mice as a present for Old Brown, and put them down upon his doorstep.

Then Twinkleberry and the other little squirrels each made a low bow, and said politely —

"Old Mr. Brown, will you favour us with permission to gather nuts upon your island?"

纳特金却表现得非常无礼,他像一颗小红樱桃似的跳上跳下,唱道:

"猜一个谜语,猜一个谜语,嘟嘟嘟!

小小的男人,红红的衣裳,嘟嘟嘟!

手拿拐杖,口含果核,嘟嘟嘟!

假如猜对了,奖你四便士,嘟嘟嘟!"

这个谜语有点老掉牙了。布朗先生根本不答理纳特金。

他固执地闭上眼睛,睡着了。

But Nutkin was excessively impertinent in his manners. He bobbed up and down like a little red *cherry*, singing —

"Riddle me, riddle me, rot-tot-tote!

A little wee man, in a red red coat!

A staff in his hand, and a stone in his throat;

If you'll tell me this riddle, I'll give you a groat."

Now this riddle is as old as the hills; Mr. Brown paid no attention whatever to Nutkin.

He shut his eyes obstinately and went to sleep.

松鼠们的小麻袋里装满了坚果。晚上他们又乘着小木筏回家去了。

The squirrels filled their little sacks with nuts, and sailed away home in the evening.

第二天早上,小松鼠们又回到了猫头鹰岛上。这次闪酱果和其他小松鼠们带来了一只漂亮的胖鼹鼠,并把它放在老布朗家门前的石头上,然后问道:

"布朗先生,您能允许我们再摘些坚果吗?"

But next morning they all came back again to Owl Island; and Twinkleberry and the others brought a fine fat mole, and laid it on the stone in front of Old Brown's doorway, and said —

"Mr. Brown, will you favour us with your gracious permission to gather some more nuts?"

然而,纳特金对布朗先生一点儿都不尊重,他又开始跳上跳下,一边用荨麻胳肢老布朗先生,一边唱道:

"老布先生!猜个谜语!

刺刺儿在墙里,

刺刺儿在墙外,

假如碰刺刺儿,

刺刺儿就咬你!"

布朗先生突然醒过来了,他抓起鼹鼠回屋去了。

But Nutkin, who had no respect, began to dance up and down, tickling old Mr. Brown with a *nettle* and singing —

"Old Mr. B! Riddle-me-ree!

Hitty Pitty within the wall,

Hitty Pitty without the wall;

If you touch Hitty Pitty,

Hitty Pitty will bite you!"

Mr. Brown woke up suddenly and carried the mole into his house.

他冲着纳特金,"砰"地把门关上。不一会儿,一缕柴火的青烟从树顶冉冉升起。纳特金一边从钥匙孔向里偷看,一边又唱起来:

"房子里满满,洞里满满,

可是碗儿装不满!"

He shut the door in Nutkin's face. Presently a little thread of blue *smoke* from a wood fire came up from the top of the tree, and Nutkin peeped through the key-hole and sang —

"A house full, a hole full!

And you cannot gather a bowl-full!"

小松鼠们在岛上四处寻找坚果，小口袋都装得满满的。

纳特金捡的却是黄色和红色的橡树籽。他坐在山毛榉的树墩上一边玩弹球，一边注视着老布朗先生的大门。

The squirrels searched for nuts all over the island and filled their little sacks.

But Nutkin gathered oak-apples — yellow and scarlet — and sat upon a beech-stump playing marbles, and watching the door of old Mr. Brown.

第三天,小松鼠们起得很早,他们出去钓鱼,抓到了七条小肥鱼,准备作为礼物送给老布朗。

他们划过湖面,在猫头鹰岛上一棵弯曲的栗树下上岸了。

On the third day the squirrels got up very early and went fishing; they caught seven fat minnows as a present for Old Brown.

They paddled over the lake and landed under a crooked chestnut tree on Owl Island.

闪酱果和其他六只小松鼠，手里都拿着一条小肥鱼。可是纳特金一点也不讲礼貌，他根本没有带礼物，却跑在前面唱道：

"荒野上的男人对我说，

　长在海里的草莓有几多？

　答案美妙你听我说，

　就像树林里长的红鱼一样多。"

即便是纳特金说出了谜底，老布朗先生对谜语仍然不感兴趣。

Twinkleberry and six other little squirrels each carried a fat minnow; but Nutkin, who had no nice manners, brought no present at all. He ran in front, singing —

"The man in the wilderness said to me,

　'How many strawberries grow in the sea?'

　I answered him as I thought good —

　'As many red herrings as grow in the wood.'"

But old Mr. Brown took no interest in riddles — not even when the answer was provided for him.

第四天，松鼠们带来的礼物是六只胖甲壳虫。对老布朗来说，这就像李子布丁里的李子一样好吃。每一只甲壳虫都精心地用酸模树叶包起来，再用一枚松针系紧。

纳特金还是和从前一样粗俗地唱着：

"老布先生！猜我一个谜语！

英国的面粉，西班牙的水果，

细雨中相会在一起，

放进袋子，系上绳子。

告诉我谜底，一只戒指送给你。"

纳特金如此夸口简直太可笑了，因为他根本没有什么戒指可以送给老布朗。

On the fourth day the squirrels brought a present of six fat beetles, which were as good as plums in *plum-pudding* for Old Brown. Each beetle was wrapped up carefully in a dock-leaf, fastened with a pine-needle pin.

But Nutkin sang as rudely as ever —

"Old Mr. B! Riddle-me-ree!

Flour of England, fruit of Spain,

Met together in a shower of rain;

Put in a bag tied round with a string,

If you'll tell me this riddle, I'll give you a ring!"

Which was ridiculous of Nutkin, because he had not got any ring to give to Old Brown.

其他松鼠在坚果灌木丛中四处搜寻,但纳特金却只顾从荆棘上捡鸫鸟的圆垫子,还在上面插满了松针。

The other squirrels hunted up and down the nut bushes; but Nutkin gathered robin's pin-cushions off a briar bush, and stuck them full of pine-needle pins.

第五天，松鼠们带来的礼物是野生蜂蜜。野生蜂蜜又甜又黏，松鼠们把它放在老布朗家门前的石头上以后，就用舌头去舔他们的手指。这蜂蜜是从山顶的野蜂巢里偷来的。

On the fifth day the squirrels brought a present of wild honey; it was so sweet and sticky that they licked their fingers as they put it down upon the stone. They had stolen it out of a bumble *bees'* nest on the tippitty top of the hill.

纳特金跳上跳下，嘴里唱道：

"嗡嗡，嗡嗡，嗡嗡叫，

我去那边捡果果，

遇到一群猪猡猡，

一些黄脖子，一些黄脊背，

他们是最漂亮的猪猡猡，

他们去过那边捡果果。"

But Nutkin skipped up and down, singing —

"Hum-a-bum! buzz! buzz! Hum-a-bum buzz!

As I went over Tipple-tine

I met a flock of bonny swine;

Some yellow-nacked, some yellow backed!

They were the very bonniest swine

That e'er went over Tipple-tine."

老布朗向上翻着白眼儿,对纳特金的傲慢无理十分厌恶。
不过,他倒是把蜂蜜全吃光了!

Old Mr. Brown turned up his eyes in disgust at the impertinence of Nutkin.

But he ate up the honey!

松鼠们的小口袋里都装满了坚果。

纳特金却坐在一块宽大平整的石板上,用山楂果和杉树果玩起了滚球游戏。

The squirrels filled their little sacks with nuts.

But Nutkin sat upon a big flat rock, and played ninepins with a crab apple and green fir-cones.

松鼠纳特金的故事
The Tale of Squirrel Nutkin

第六天是周六,松鼠们最后一次来到小岛。他们带来了一个新下的鸡蛋,用小蒲筐装着,作为给老布朗最后的告别礼物。

纳特金跑在前面,又是笑,又是喊:

"小溪里躺着驼胖墩,

　脖子上围着白床单,

　医生工匠各四十,

　也矫正不了驼胖墩!"

On the sixth day, which was Saturday, the squirrels came again for the last time; they brought a new-laid *egg* in a little rush basket as a last parting present for Old Brown.

But Nutkin ran in front laughing, and shouting —

"Humpty Dumpty lies in the beck,

　With a white counterpane round his neck,

　Forty doctors and forty wrights,

　Cannot put Humpty Dumpty to rights!"

老布朗先生对蛋有些兴趣。他睁开一只眼睛,又闭上了,还是什么话也没有说。

Now old Mr. Brown took an interest in eggs; he opened one eye and shut it again. But still he did not speak.

松鼠纳特金的故事
The Tale of Squirrel Nutkin

纳特金变得更加粗鲁不敬 ——

"老布先生！老布先生！

马笼头，马勒绳，

挂在国王的厨房门上！

国王的宝马和卫士，

都取不走挂在国王厨房门上的

马笼头，马勒绳！"

他像一道阳光，在老布朗眼前晃来晃去，可是老布朗依然什么话也没说。

Nutkin became more and more impertinent —

"Old Mr.B! Old Mr.B!

Hickamore, Hackamore,

on the King's kitchen door;

All the King's horses,

and all the King's men,

Couldn't drive Hickamore, Hackamore,

Off the King's kitchen door!"

Nutkin danced up and down like a *sunbeam*; but still Old Brown said nothing at all.

纳特金又开始唱道:

"亚瑟·奥鲍尔搞断了他的戒指,

他咆哮着来到这块土地!

苏格兰王竭尽全力,

亚瑟·奥鲍尔也没有离去!"

他发出了"呼呼"声,听起来就像刮风的声音。他一路疾跑,竟然一下子跳到了老布朗的头上!

……紧接着,只听见一阵扑腾和扭打声,然后是一声尖叫"哎呀"!其他松鼠吓得纷纷逃进了灌木丛。

Nutkin began again —

"Arthur O'Bower has broken his band,

He comes roaring up the land!

The King of Scots with all his power,

Cannot turn Arthur of the Bower!"

Nutkin made a whirring noise to sound like the *wind*, and he took a running jump right onto the head of Old Brown!...

Then all at once there was a flutterment and a scufflement and a loud "Squeak!"

The other squirrels scuttered away into the bushes.

当松鼠们小心翼翼地从灌木丛里探身出来,偷偷地向那棵树周围张望时,只看见老布朗坐在门槛上,动也不动,双眼紧闭,好像什么事也没有发生过。

*

可是,纳特金已经被抓进了他的腰包里!

When they came back very cautiously, peeping round the tree — there was Old Brown sitting on his door-step, quite still, with his eyes closed, as if nothing had happened.

*

But Nutkin was in his waist-coat pocket!

到这里,故事好像已经结束了。其实呀,还没有完!

This looks like the end of the story; but it isn't.

老布朗把纳特金带进了家里,抓住他的尾巴,把他拎起来,打算剥他的皮。纳特金拼命挣扎,结果他的尾巴断成了两截儿。他猛地冲上楼梯,从阁楼的窗户逃了出去。

Old Brown carried Nutkin into his house, and held him up by the tail, intending to skin him;but Nutkin pulled so very hard that his tail broke in two, and he dashed up the staircase, and escaped out of the attic window.

松鼠纳特金的故事
The Tale of Squirrel Nutkin

时至今日,如果你见到纳特金在树上,而让他猜谜语的话,他会向你扔树枝,然后跺脚大骂,高喊:"滚!滚开!快滚开!"

(完)

And to this day, if you meet Nutkin up a tree and ask him a riddle, he will throw sticks at you, and stamp his feet and scold, and shout —

"Cuck-cuck-cuck-cur-r-r-cuck-k-k!"

THE END

小猪鲁滨逊的故事

The Tale of Little Pig Robinson

1930

第一章

　　我小时候，总是去海边度假。住在一个小镇上，那儿有海港、渔船和渔民。渔民们扬帆去远航，拉网捕鲱鱼。等渔船返航归来，有的渔民只捕到几条鲱鱼，有的渔民却捕到许多鲱鱼，以至于无法全部卸到码头上。于是，就有一些马拉着大车蹚着海水到浅滩去迎接满载的船只。鱼从船的一侧被铲进大车上，然后，被送往火车站，装进运鱼专列，送往大城市。

Chapter One

When I was a child I used to go to the seaside for the holidays. We stayed in a little town where there was a harbour and fishing boats and fishermen. They sailed away to catch herrings in nets. When the boats came back home again some had only caught a few herrings. Others had caught so many that they could not all be unloaded on to the quay. Then horses and carts were driven into the shallow water at low tide to meet the heavily laden boats. The fish were shovelled over the side of the boat into the carts, and taken to the railway station, where a special train of fish trucks was waiting.

每当渔船满载而归的时候，人们总是兴奋不已。镇上一半的人，包括猫，都会跑到码头迎接。

一只名叫苏珊的白猫从不错过每次机会。她是老渔夫萨姆的太太贝齐的猫。贝齐患有风湿病，没有孩子，只有苏珊和五只母鸡。贝齐坐在壁炉旁，腰背疼痛，每次加煤和搅动罐里东西的时候，她都会发出吃力的声音："噢！噢！"苏珊坐在贝齐对面，她为贝齐感到难过。她真希望知道怎样加煤和搅动锅里的东西。萨姆外出捕鱼的时候，她们就从早到晚坐在壁炉旁，喝杯茶和一些牛奶。

Great was the excitement when the fishing boats returned with a good catch of herrings. Half the people in the town ran down to the quay, including cats.

There was a white cat called Susan who never missed meeting the boats. She belonged to the wife of an old fisherman named Sam. The wife's name was Betsy. She had rheumatics, and she had no family except Susan and five hens. Betsy sat by the fire; her back ached; she said "Ow! Ow!" whenever she had to put coal on, and stir the pot. Susan sat opposite to Betsy. She felt sorry for Betsy; she wished she knew how to put the coal on and stir the pot. All day long they sat by the fire, while Sam was away fishing. They had a cup of tea and some milk.

贝齐说:"苏珊,我都快要站不起来了,你到前门去,等候主人的船吧。"

"Susan," said Betsy, "I can hardly stand up. Go to the front gate and look out for Master's boat."

苏珊去了又回来,来回走了三四次。黄昏时分,她终于看到船队的桅帆从远处的海面驶过来。

"苏珊,拿上我的篮子到港口去,向主人要六条鲱鱼,我要拿它做晚餐。"

苏珊拿了篮子,向贝齐借了无边小圆软帽和小彩格呢披肩。我看见她急急忙忙地赶往港口。

其他猫也从农舍里走出来,顺着通往海滨的斜坡路跑去。到那里去的还有鸭子,我觉得他们的顶冠最奇特了,就像苏格兰人戴的宽边圆帽似的。几乎每个人都急忙赶去迎接船只。而我却碰到一只

Susan went out and came back. Three or four times she went out into the garden. At last, late in the afternoon, she saw the sails of the fishing fleet, coming in over the sea.

"Go down to the harbour; ask Master for six herrings; I will cook them for supper. Take my basket, Susan."

Susan took the basket; also she borrowed Betsy's bonnet and little plaid shawl. I saw her hurrying down to the harbour.

Other cats were coming out of the cottages, and running down the steep streets that lead to the sea front. Also ducks. I remember that they were most peculiar ducks with top-knots that looked like tam-o'-shanter caps. Everybody was hurrying to meet the boats — nearly everybody. I only met one person, a dog called Stumpy, who was going the opposite

叫斯达姆比的狗,向对面的路上走去,嘴里还衔着一个纸口袋。

有些狗不喜欢吃鱼。斯达姆比去了肉店给自己、鲍勃、珀西和罗西小姐买羊排骨。斯达姆比是只认真、守规矩的短尾大棕狗。他和猎犬鲍勃、珀西猫和管家罗西小姐住在一起。斯达姆比曾是一位老富绅的狗,老富绅去世后,给斯达姆比留了一笔钱——每周十先令,直到斯达姆比过世。这就是为什么斯达姆比、鲍勃和珀西猫都住在一所美丽的小房子里的原因。

苏珊提着篮子在宽街的拐角处碰到了斯达姆比,苏珊行了个屈膝礼。如果她不是急着要接船,她会停下来打听一下珀西的情况的。

way. He was carrying a paper parcel in his mouth.

Some dogs do not care for fish. Stumpy had been to the butcher's to buy mutton chops for himself and Bob and Percy and Miss Rose. Stumpy was a large, serious, well-behaved brown dog with a short tail. He lived with Bob the retriever and Percy the cat and Miss Rose who kept house. Stumpy had belonged to a very rich old gentleman; and when the old gentleman died he left money to Stumpy — ten shillings a week for the rest of Stumpy's life. So that was why Stumpy and Bob and Percy the cat all lived together in a pretty little house.

Susan with her basket met Stumpy at the corner of Broad Street. Susan made a curtsy. She would have stopped to inquire after Percy, only she was in a hurry to meet the boat.

珀西的腿瘸了,是被奶车车轮碾坏的。

斯达姆比没有停下来,他从眼角向苏珊瞄了一眼,摇了摇尾巴。他既不能鞠躬,也不能说"下午好",要不他嘴里的那包羊排就会掉下来。他从宽街出来,拐进伍德拜因巷,他就住在那里。他推开大门,走进了一所房子里。不久,一股饭香从屋里飘出来,我相信斯达姆比、鲍勃和罗西小姐肯定喜欢吃羊排。

吃晚饭的时候,珀西不见了,他从窗户溜出去,和镇上的其他猫一样,去迎接渔船了。

Percy was lame; he had hurt his foot. It had been trapped under the wheel of a milk cart.

Stumpy looked at Susan out of the corner of his eye; he wagged his tail, but he did not stop. He could not bow or say "good afternoon" for fear of dropping the parcel of mutton chops. He turned out of Broad Street into Woodbine Lane, where he lived; he pushed open the front door and disappeared into a house. Presently there was a smell of cooking, and I have no doubt that Stumpy and Bob and Miss Rose enjoyed their mutton chops.

Percy could not be found at dinner-time. He had slipped out of the window, and, like all the other cats in the town, he had gone to meet the fishing boats.

苏珊沿着宽街赶路,她走下很陡的台阶,抄小道去港口。鸭子们很机灵,他们走另一条路。因为台阶对任何脚不利索的人都太陡,太滑,而作为猫的苏珊轻而易举地就下去了。在房子高高的后墙之间有 43 个台阶,它们既黑暗又泥泞。

绳索和松香的气味以及嘈杂的声音从下面传上来。台阶的底部就是码头。

潮退了,水没有了,船只停在烂泥上。有几只船停靠在码头边,其他的船停泊在防洪堤墙内。

Susan hurried along Broad Street and took the short cut to the harbour, down a steep flight of steps. The ducks had wisely gone another way, round by the sea front. The steps were too steep and slippery for anyone less sure-footed than a cat. Susan went down quickly and easily. There were forty-three steps, rather dark and slimy, between high backs of houses.

A smell of ropes and pitch and a good deal of noise came up from below. At the bottom of the steps was the quay, or landing place, beside the inner harbour.

The tide was out; there was no water; the vessels rested on the dirty mud. Several ships were moored beside the quay; others were anchored inside the breakwater.

在台阶旁边，两艘脏兮兮的运煤船在卸煤，一艘是森德兰市的"马乔里·道"号，另一艘是加的夫市的"珍妮·琼斯"号。男人们推着一车又一车煤在木板上飞跑。岸上的吊车摆动着煤斗，卸下煤斗里的煤，发出一阵阵"隆隆"的响声。

码头的另一侧，一艘"坎德尔斯的庞德"号正往船上装杂货。一捆又一捆，一桶又一桶，一箱又一箱——各式各样的货物被装进了船舱。水手和装卸工们叫喊着，铁链碰撞发出"嘎嘎"声和"当当"声。苏珊找了个机会悄悄地穿过嘈杂的人群。她看到一桶苹果

Near the steps, coal was being unloaded from two grimy colliers called the "Margery Dawe" of Sunderland, and the "Jenny Jones" of Cardiff. Men ran along planks with wheelbarrowfuls of coal; coal scoops were swung ashore by cranes, and emptied with loud thumping and rattling.

Farther along the quay, another ship called the "Pound of Candles" was taking a mixed cargo on board. Bales, casks, packing-cases, barrels — all manner of goods were being stowed into the hold; sailors and stevedores shouted; chains rattled and clanked. Susan waited for an opportunity to slip past the noisy crowd. She watched a cask of cider that bobbed

酒在空中上下摆动，正从码头移往"坎德尔斯的庞德"号的甲板上。一只黄猫坐在帆索上，也在盯着那只桶。

粗绳通过滑轮慢慢移动，苹果酒桶晃晃悠悠地滑到甲板上。水手在下面说：

"留神！小心你的头，年轻的先生！别挡着路！"

"哼，哼，哼！"一只粉色小猪哼叫着，在"坎德尔斯的庞德"号甲板上惊慌地四处跑动。

帆索上的黄猫看了看小粉猪，又看了看码头那边的苏珊，眼睛一眨一眨的。

and swung in the air, on its passage from the quay to the deck of the "Pound of Candles". A yellow cat who sat in the rigging was also watching the cask.

The rope ran through the pulley; the cask went down bobbitty on to the deck, where a sailor man was waiting for it. Said the sailor down below:

"Look out! Mind your head, young sir! Stand out of the way!"

"Wee, wee, wee!" grunted a small pink pig, scampering round the deck of the "Pound of Candles".

The yellow cat in the rigging watched the small pink pig. The yellow cat in the rigging looked across at Susan on the quay. The yellow cat winked.

苏珊看见一只猪在船上,觉得很奇怪,但是她正忙着赶路,没时间理会这些。她顺着码头往前挤过去。码头上乱哄哄的:成堆的煤、一辆辆吊车、推着手推车的男人们、"嗡嗡嗡"的嘈杂声和各种各样刺鼻的气味。她走过鱼市、鱼箱子、分鱼工人,还有女人们正在往里装鲱鱼和盐的一排排的鱼桶。

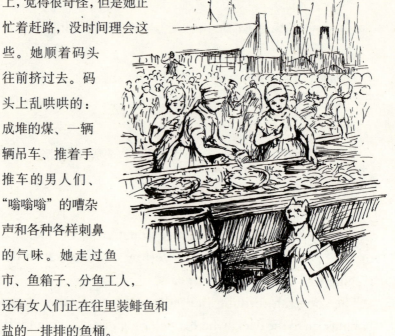

Susan was surprised to see a pig on board a ship. But she was in a hurry. She threaded her way along the quay, amongst coal and cranes, and men wheeling hand-trucks, and noises, and smells. She passed the fish auction, and fish boxes, and fish sorters, and barrels that women were filling with herrings and salt.

海鸥俯冲下来,发出尖叫声。上百个鱼箱和成吨的鲜鱼被装进小轮船的船舱。苏珊很庆幸自己终于挤出了人群,她沿着一小段台阶,来到外港的岸边。不一会儿,鸭子们也一摇一摆、"嘎嘎"叫着走来了。而老萨姆的船 ——"贝齐·蒂明斯"号,也是鲱鱼船队的最后一条船,满满的,沉沉的,绕过防洪堤驶进港来,那粗钝的船鼻直插进铺满小卵石的海滩。

萨姆满载而归,兴高采烈。他和他的伙伴,还有两个小伙子开始把鱼卸到手推车上。因为潮水太低了,渔船上又满载着鲱鱼,使它无法驶进码头。

Seagulls swooped and screamed. Hundreds of fish boxes and tons of fresh fish were being loaded into the hold of a small steamer. Susan was glad to get away from the crowd, down a much shorter flight of steps on to the shore of the outer harbour. The ducks arrived soon afterwards, waddling and quacking. And old Sam's boat, the "Betsy Timmins", last of the herring fleet and heavy laden, came in round the breakwater; and drove her blunt nose into the shingle.

Sam was in high spirits; he had had a big catch. He and his mate and two lads commenced to unload their fish into carts, as the tide was too low to float the fishing boat up to the quay. The boat was full of herrings.

但是，不管运气好坏，萨姆总是扔一把鲱鱼给苏珊。

"这是送给两位老小姐的，做一顿热乎乎的晚餐！接住，苏珊！要老实哟！这条破鱼给你！把其他的鱼给贝齐。"

鸭子正在游水觅食，贪婪地吃着。海鸥尖叫着，不时地俯冲下来。苏珊提着一篮鲱鱼，爬上台阶，从后街回家了。

老贝齐给她自己和苏珊烧了两条鱼，另外两条鱼留给萨姆回来当晚饭。然后，她拿上用绒布衬裙裹好的治风湿病的热水袋，睡觉去了。

But, good luck or bad luck, Sam never failed to throw a handful of herrings to Susan.

"Here's for the two old girls and a hot supper! Catch them, Susan! Honest now! Here's a broken fish for you! Now take the others to Betsy."

The ducks were dabbling and gobbling; the seagulls were screaming and swooping. Susan climbed the steps with her basket of herrings and went home by back streets.

Old Betsy cooked two herrings for herself and Susan, another two for Sam's supper when he came in. Then she went to bed with a hot bottle wrapped in a flannel petticoat to help her rheumatics.

萨姆吃完晚饭,坐在壁炉前抽了一袋烟,也去睡觉了。但苏珊却在壁炉前坐了很久,想了许多事情——鱼、鸭子、瘸腿珀西、吃羊排骨的狗、船上的黄猫和小粉猪。苏珊觉得在"坎德尔斯的庞德"号船上看到的那只小猪很奇怪。这时候,老鼠们在碗橱门儿下面探头探脑地朝外张望。煤渣从炉子里掉了出来。苏珊想着想着睡着了,还发出一串串轻微的呼噜声。她梦见了鱼和猪,她无法理解猪怎么会在船上。但是,我知道有关猪的一切。

Sam ate his supper and smoked a pipe by the fire; and then he went to bed. But Susan sat a long time by the fire, considering. She considered many things — fish, and ducks, and Percy with a lame foot, and dogs that eat mutton chops, and the yellow cat on the ship, and the pig. Susan thought it strange to see a pig upon a ship called the "Pound of Candles". The mice peeped out under the cupboard door. The cinders fell together on the hearth. Susan purred gently in her sleep and dreamed of fish and pigs. She could not understand that pig on board a ship. But I know all about him!

第二章

你还记得关于猫头鹰和猫咪以及美丽青豆色船的那首歌吗?他们是怎样拿到蜂蜜和好多的钱,并把它们包在一张五英镑的钞票里的?

一年零一天,他们扬帆远航,
来到蓬树生长的地方——
在树林里,站着一只小猪,
指环挂在鼻尖上,
指环挂在鼻尖上。

Chapter Two

You remember the song about the Owl and the Pussy Cat and their beautiful pea-green boat? How they took some honey and plenty of money, wrapped up in a five pound note?

They sailed away, for a year and a day,
To the land where the Bong tree grows —
And, there in a wood, a piggy-wig stood,
With a ring at the end of his nose — his nose,
With a ring at the end of his nose.

现在，我要给你讲那只猪的故事，为什么他会住在蓬树生长的地方。

这只猪小的时候和他的两个姨妈——多克斯小姐和波克斯小姐，住在德文夏一座叫做皮戈瑞·波康比的农场里。他们舒适的茅屋坐落在一个果园里，一条红色陡峭的小道直通到那儿。

那里的土壤是红色的，草是绿色的。从上面远远望下去，她们可以看到红色的悬崖和少许淡蓝色的海洋。船扬起白帆航行在海面上，驶进斯蒂茅斯港。

Now I am going to tell you the story of that pig, and why he went to live in the land of the Bong tree.

When that pig was little he lived in Devonshire, with his aunts, Miss Dorcas and Miss Porcas, at a farm called Piggery Porcombe. Their cosy thatched cottage was in an orchard at the top of a steep red Devonshire lane.

The soil was red, the grass was green; and far away below in the distance they could see red cliffs and a bit of bright blue sea. Ships with white sails sailed over the sea into the harbour of Stymouth.

我曾经常提到，德文夏的农场有很多奇怪的名字。假如你看过皮戈瑞·波康比，你会认为住在那儿的人也非常古怪！多克斯姨妈是一头杂色肥猪，养了很多母鸡。波克斯姨妈是一头笑容满面的大块头黑猪，平时替人洗衣服。在这个故事里，我们不会听到太多有关她们的事情。她们过着富裕、平静的生活，而她们的结局是被做成熏肉。但她们的外甥鲁滨逊却有过极不寻常的冒险经历。

小猪鲁滨逊是个挺可爱的小家伙，皮肤白里透红，一双小小的蓝眼睛，胖脸蛋儿，双下巴，小翘鼻，翘鼻上挂着一只纯银的指环。

I have often remarked that the Devonshire farms have very strange names. If you had ever seen Piggery Porcombe you would think that the people who lived there were very queer too! Aunt Dorcas was a stout speckled pig who kept hens. Aunt Porcas was a large smiling black pig who took in washing. We shall not hear very much about them in this story. They led prosperous uneventful lives, and their end was bacon. But their nephew Robinson had the most peculiar adventures that ever happened to a pig.

Little pig Robinson was a charming little fellow; pinky white with small blue eyes, fat cheeks and a double chin, and a turned-up nose, with a real silver ring in it. Robinson could

如果鲁滨逊闭上一只眼,眯着另一只眼侧视,就能看见那只指环。

鲁滨逊总是很满足,很愉快。他成天在农场里乱跑,自己哼着小曲,咕哝着:"噢,噢,噢!"鲁滨逊走了以后,姨妈们还伤感地思念着那些小曲呢!

see that ring if he shut one eye and squinted sideways.

He was always contented and happy. All day long he ran about the farm, singing little songs to himself, and grunting "Wee, wee, wee!" His aunts missed those little songs sadly after Robinson had left them.

有人和鲁滨逊说话的时候,他总是回答:"噢?噢?噢?"他听的时候,把头歪到一边,眯起一只眼睛,"噢?噢?噢?"

鲁滨逊的老姨妈们喂养他,照顾他,同时也让他忙个不停。

"鲁滨逊!鲁滨逊!"多克斯姨妈叫道,"快来!我听见有只母鸡在'咯哒咯哒'地叫了。去把鸡蛋给我捡回来,别弄破了!"

"噢,噢,噢!"鲁滨逊像一个小法国人那样回答。

波克斯姨妈从晾衣服的草地上喊道:"鲁滨逊!鲁滨逊!我掉

"Wee? Wee? Wee?" he answered when anybody spoke to him. "Wee? Wee? Wee?" listening with his head on one side and one eye screwed up.

Robinson's old aunts fed him and petted him and kept him on the trot.

"Robinson! Robinson!" called Aunt Dorcas. "Come quick! I hear a hen clucking. Fetch me the egg; don't break it now!"

"Wee, wee, wee!" answered Robinson, like a little Frenchman.

"Robinson! Robinson! I've dropped a clothes peg, come

了一个衣服夹子,快来给我捡起来!"(她简直是太胖了,无法弯下腰来捡任何东西)。

鲁滨逊回答道:"噢,噢,噢!"

两个姨妈都非常、非常壮实,而在斯蒂茅斯周围地区,那些翻越围栏的梯子都很窄。从皮戈瑞·波康比过来的小道穿过许多的田地,这是在绿草和雏菊之间被行人踩出来的红色小道。在小道从一个农场通向另一个农场的地方,一定会有翻越篱笆围栏的梯子。

and pick it up for me!" called Aunt Porcas from the drying green (she being almost too fat to stoop down and pick up anything).

"Wee, wee, wee!" answered Robinson.

Both the aunts were very, very stout. And the stiles in the neighbourhood of Stymouth are narrow. The footpath from Piggery Porcombe crosses many fields; a red trodden track between short green grass and daisies. And wherever the footpath crosses over from one field to another field, there is sure to be a stile in the hedge.

"不是我太壮实,而是那些梯子太单薄。"多克斯姨妈对波克斯姨妈说,"如果我待在家里,你能从那梯子上挤过去吗?"

"我可不行,两年前就不行了。"波克斯姨妈回答道。"真叫人恼火,那个搬运工真让人恼火,就在赶集的前一天,他把驴车给弄翻了。一打鸡蛋可是两便士呢!从大路绕着走,而不穿过田地,你估计要走多远?"

"如果是一趟,就是四英里。"波克斯姨妈叹了口气说,"我的肥皂就剩下最后一点了。无论如何我们得买点东西吧?那头驴子说,修好那辆大车得需要一个星期。"

"It is not me that is too stout; it is the stiles that are too thin," said Aunt Dorcas to Aunt Porcas. "Could you manage to squeeze through them if I stayed at home?"

"I could *not*. Not for two years I could *not*," replied Aunt Porcas. "Aggravating, it *is* aggravating of that carrier man, to go and upset his donkey cart the day before market day. And eggs at two and tuppence a dozen! How far do you call it to walk all the way round by the road instead of crossing the fields?"

"Four miles if it's one," sighed Aunt Porcas, "and me using my last bit of soap. However will we get our shopping done? The donkey says the cart will take a week to mend."

"如果你在晚饭前去,你是不是就可以挤过梯子了?"

"不行,我不行,我会卡得死死的,你也会被卡住的。"波克斯姨妈说。

多克斯姨妈开始说:"你不认为我们可以冒险 —— "

"冒险让鲁滨逊从小路去斯蒂茅斯?"波克斯姨妈接着把话说完。

"噢,噢,噢!"鲁滨逊回答道。

"尽管他的身材大小合适,可我不愿意让他一个人去。"

"Don't you think you could squeeze through the stiles if you went before dinner?"

"No, I don't, I would stick fast; and so would you," said Aunt Porcas.

"Don't you think we might venture —" commenced Aunt Dorcas.

"Venture to send Robinson by the footpath to Stymouth?" finished Aunt Porcas.

"Wee, wee, wee!" answered Robinson.

"I scarcely like to send him alone, though he is sensible for his size."

"噢，噢，噢！"鲁滨逊回答道。

"但是，我们也没有其他办法啊！"多克斯姨妈说。

她们把鲁滨逊和剩下的一点肥皂放进了澡盆。经过刷洗、擦干、擦光，他就像一根新别针那样光亮。接着，她们给鲁滨逊穿上蓝布连衣裙和短衬裤，然后吩咐他带上一个大菜篮子去斯蒂茅斯购物。

在篮子里有两打鸡蛋、一捆黄水仙花、两个春天的菜花，还有鲁滨逊的晚饭——果酱三明治。他必须在集市上卖掉那些鸡蛋、花和蔬菜，然后买回各种各样的商品。

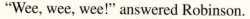

"Wee, wee, wee!" answered Robinson.

"But there is nothing else to be done," said Aunt Dorcas.

So Robinson was popped into the wash-tub with the last bit of soap. He was scrubbed and dried and polished as bright as a new pin. Then he was dressed in a little blue cotton frock and knickers, and instructed to go shopping to Stymouth with a big market basket.

In the basket were two dozen eggs, a bunch of daffodils, two spring cauliflowers; also Robinson's dinner of bread-and-jam sandwiches. The eggs and flowers and vegetables he must sell in the market, and bring back various other purchases from shopping.

"好了,在斯蒂茅斯,你要好好照顾自己,鲁滨逊。当心火药、船上的厨师、仓库、香肠、鞋子、船只、火漆。别忘了买蓝纸口袋、肥皂、织补的毛线 —— 还有什么来着?"多克斯姨妈说。

"织补的毛线、肥皂、蓝纸袋、酵母 —— 还有一个什么来着?"波克斯姨妈说。

"噢,噢,噢!"鲁滨逊回答道。

"Now take care of yourself in Stymouth, Nephew Robinson. Beware of gunpowder, and ships' cooks, and pantechnicons, and sausages, and shoes, and ships, and sealing-wax. Remember the blue bag, the soap, the darning wool — what was the other thing?" said Aunt Dorcas.

"The darning wool, the soap, the blue bag, the yeast — what was the other thing?" said Aunt Porcas.

"Wee, wee, wee!" answered Robinson.

"蓝纸口袋、肥皂、酵母、织补的毛线、圆白菜种子 —— 这是五样,应该有六样。这比四个多了两个,因为手绢四角只能结四个结,这就多出来两个,就用这种办法记。买六件东西,它应该是 —— "

波克斯姨妈说:"想起来了,是茶叶。茶叶、蓝纸袋、肥皂、织补的毛线、酵母、圆白菜种子,一共六样东西。大部分可以到芒比先生的店里买。鲁滨逊,向他解释一下关于搬运工的事,告诉他下个星期我们会给他带去洗好的衣服和更多的蔬菜。"

"The blue bag, the soap, the yeast, the darning wool, the cabbage seed — that's five, and there ought to be six. It was two more than four because it was two too many to tie knots in the corners of his hankie, to remember by. Six to buy, it should be —"

"I have it!" said Aunt Porcas. "It was tea — tea, blue bag, soap, darning wool, yeast, cabbage seed. You will buy most of them at Mr. Mumby's. Explain about the carrier, Robinson; tell him we will bring the washing and some more vegetables next week."

"噢，噢，噢！"鲁滨逊回答道，然后拿着大菜篮出发了。

多克斯姨妈和波克斯姨妈站在门廊里，望着他安全地离去，走向田地，爬过第一个翻越围栏的梯子，直到看不见他为止。当她们回去做家务的时候，她们互相没好气儿地嚷嚷，因为她们都很为鲁滨逊担忧。

"不让他去就好了，你和你那个讨厌的蓝纸袋！"多克斯姨妈说。

"Wee, wee, wee!" answered Robinson, setting off with the big basket.

Aunt Dorcas and Aunt Porcas stood in the porch. They watched him safely out of sight, down the field, and through the first of the many stiles. When they went back to their household tasks they were grunty and snappy with each other, because they were uneasy about Robinson.

"I wish we had not let him go. You and your tiresome blue bag!" said Aunt Dorcas.

"蓝纸袋,对呀!还有你的毛线和鸡蛋!"波克斯姨妈抱怨地说,"让那个搬运工和他的驴车见鬼去吧!他怎么不能在赶集以前躲开那条沟呢?"

"Blue bag, indeed! It was your darning wool and eggs!" grumbled Aunt Porcas. "Bother that carrier man and his donkey cart! Why could not he keep out of the ditch until after market day?"

第三章

即使抄小路走到斯蒂茅斯，路还是很远。好在一路都是下坡，鲁滨逊喜气洋洋的。早上天气很好，他高兴地唱起小曲子："噢，噢，噢！"云雀也在他头顶歌唱。

高高的蓝天上，回旋着海鸥白色的身影，嘶哑的叫声从遥远的高空徐徐飘来，竟变得柔和了。高傲的白嘴鸦和活泼的寒鸦在雏菊

Chapter Three

The walk to Stymouth was a long one, in spite of going by the fields. But the footpath ran downhill all the way, and Robinson was merry. He sang his little song, for joy of the fine morning, and he chuckled "Wee, wee, wee!" Larks were singing, too, high overhead.

And higher still — high up against blue sky, the great white gulls sailed in wide circles. Their hoarse cries came softened back to earth from a great way up above. Important rooks and

小猪鲁滨逊的故事
The Tale of Little Pig Robinson

和毛茛的草坪上昂首阔步。小羊蹦蹦跳跳,"咩咩"地叫着。山羊掉头看着鲁滨逊,慈爱地说:

"小猪,在斯蒂茅斯要小心照顾自己。"

鲁滨逊一路小跑,累得上气不接下气,全身发热。他穿过五座农庄,攀过数不清的围栏——有台阶的围栏、梯状围栏、木桩围栏,有的围栏是一个很重的筐子,非常别扭。当他回过头来,皮戈瑞·波康比农场已经看不到了。在他前面很远的地方,在农田和峭壁那边——深蓝的大海波浪滔天。

lively jackdaws strutted about the meadows amongst the daisies and buttercups. Lambs skipped and baa'ed; the sheep looked round at Robinson.

"Mind yourself in Stymouth, little pig," said a motherly ewe.

Robinson trotted on until he was out of breath and very hot. He had crossed five big fields, and ever so many stiles; stiles with steps; ladder stiles; stiles of wooden posts; some of them were very awkward with a heavy basket. The farm of Piggery Porcombe was no longer in sight when he looked back. In the distance before him, beyond the farmlands and cliffs — never any nearer — the dark blue sea rose like a wall.

鲁滨逊在遮阳的篱笆旁坐下休息,在他的上方,白色柳絮在绽放,堤岸上布满了上千朵樱草花,暖融融的青苔和青草的香味以及潮湿的红土地蒸腾的气味弥漫在空气之中。

"如果我现在把晚饭吃了,我就不用提着了。噢,噢,噢!"鲁滨逊说。

走了这一大段路之后,他已是饥肠辘辘,他特别想在吃完果酱三明治后再吃一个鸡蛋,但他很有教养,没有这样做。

"如果那样就不够两打了。"鲁滨逊说。

Robinson sat down to rest beside a hedge in a sheltered sunny spot. Yellow pussy willow catkins were in flower above his head; there were primroses in hundreds on the bank, and a warm smell of moss and grass and steaming moist red earth.

"If I eat my dinner now, I will not have to carry it. Wee, wee, wee!" said Robinson.

The walk had made him so hungry he would have liked to eat an egg as well as the jam sandwiches; but he had been too well brought up.

"It would spoil the two dozen," said Robinson.

他摘了一把樱草花，用毛线把它们捆起来，毛线是多克斯姨妈给他做样子的。

"我要在集市上把它们卖了，攒点儿钱，用我的几个便士买些糖。我一共有多少便士？"鲁滨逊说着，摸了摸他的口袋，"一便士是多克斯姨妈给的，一便士是波克斯姨妈给的，还有一便士是卖樱草花赚的。噢，噢，噢！有人在小路上跑呢，我赶集要晚了！"

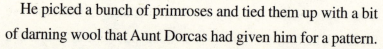

He picked a bunch of primroses and tied them up with a bit of darning wool that Aunt Dorcas had given him for a pattern.
"I will sell them in the market for my very own self, and buy sweeties with my pennies. How many pennies have I got?" said Robinson, feeling in his pocket. "One from Aunt Dorcas, and one from Aunt Porcas, and one for my primroses for my very own self — oh, wee, wee, wee! There is somebody trotting along the road! I shall be late for market!"

鲁滨逊跳起来,顺着狭窄的围栏梯子把他的篮子移过去。这里的小道和大马路交叉着连接在一起。他看到一个人骑着马,那是老佩珀雷尔先生。他骑着一匹栗色的白腿马过来了,两只高大的猎犬跑在他的前头。他们越过围栏,跳跃着来到鲁滨逊跟前。他们身材高大,看上去很友好。他们舔着鲁滨逊的脸蛋,问他篮子里装了什么东西。佩珀雷尔先生大声地叫他们回去。

Robinson jumped up and pushed his basket through a very narrow stile, where the footpath crossed into the public road. He saw a man on horseback. Old Mr. Pepperil came up, riding a chestnut horse with white legs. His two tall greyhounds ran before him; they looked through the bars of the gates into every field that they passed. They came bounding up to Robinson, very large and friendly; they licked his face and asked what he had got in that basket. Mr. Pepperil called them.

"过来,派瑞特!过来,泼斯特博伊!到这儿来,老兄!"佩珀雷尔可不想赔那些鸡蛋。

这条路新近铺上了尖硬的小碎石。佩珀雷尔先生在草地边上遛他的栗色马,和鲁滨逊聊起天来。他是一位快活的老绅士,红红的脸,白色的连鬓胡,很是和蔼可亲。斯蒂茅斯和皮戈瑞·波康比之间的绿色田野和红土耕地都属于他。

"Here, Pirate! Here, Postboy! Come here, sir!" He did not wish to be answerable for the eggs.

The road had been recently covered with sharp new flints. Mr. Pepperil walked the chestnut horse on the grass edge, and talked to Robinson. He was a jolly old gentleman, very affable, with a red face and white whiskers. All the green fields and red ploughland between Stymouth and Piggery Porcombe belonged to him.

"你好！你去哪儿呀，小猪鲁滨逊？"

"噢，佩珀雷尔先生，我去集市。噢，噢，噢！"鲁滨逊说。

"怎么，就你自己？多克斯小姐和波克斯小姐在哪儿？我想，她们没有病吧？"

"Hullo, hullo! And where are you off to, little pig Robinson?"

"Please, Mr. Pepperil, sir, I'm going to market. Wee, wee, wee!" said Robinson.

"What, all by yourself? Where are Miss Dorcas and Miss Porcas? Not ill, I trust?"

鲁滨逊向他解释关于围栏旁的木梯子太窄的事。

"哎呀，哎呀！太胖了，太胖啦？所以你就一个人去了？你姨妈为什么不养一条狗为她们跑腿？"

鲁滨逊通情达理地回答了佩珀雷尔先生所有的问题。对于这么年轻的小猪来说，他显得很有灵性，而且对蔬菜有着丰富的知识。他几乎就在马身下跟着跑，抬起头就能看见马锃亮的皮毛、宽宽的白肚带和佩珀雷尔先生的皮腿套和棕色的皮靴。佩珀雷尔先生对鲁滨逊很满意，给了他一个便士。到了新铺的燧石路的尽头，佩珀雷尔先生收紧缰绳，用脚后跟碰了碰马，就上路了。

Robinson explained about the narrow stiles.

"Dear, dear! Too fat, too fat? So you are going all alone? Why don't your aunts keep a dog to run errands?"

Robinson answered all Mr. Pepperil's questions very sensibly and prettily. He showed much intelligence, and quite a good knowledge of vegetables, for one so young. He trotted along almost under the horse, looking up at its shiny chestnut coat, and the broad white girth, and Mr. Pepperil's gaiters and brown leather boots. Mr. Pepperil was pleased with Robinson; he gave him another penny. At the end of the flints, he gathered up the reins and touched the horse with his heel.

"那么,再见,小猪。代我向你的姨妈们问好。在斯蒂茅斯,你自己要当心。"他吹哨召回他的狗,然后就骑着马离开了。

鲁滨逊沿着这条路继续往前走。他经过一个果园,看见七头又瘦又脏的猪在那里觅食,他们的鼻子上可没有银指环!鲁滨逊穿过斯泰佛得桥,他并没有停步从桥的矮挡墙往下看小鱼儿,它们正逆流而上,在缓慢的水流中尽力保持平衡;也没有停下来去看那些在漂浮的水草中戏水觅食的白鸭。鲁滨逊拜访了斯蒂茅斯磨坊,替多克斯姨妈给磨坊主捎了个口信,告诉他关于燕麦片的事。磨坊主的太太给了他一个苹果。

"Well, good day, little pig. Kind regards to the aunts. Mind yourself in Stymouth." He whistled for his dogs, and trotted away.

Robinson continued to walk along the road. He passed by an orchard where seven thin dirty pigs were grubbing. They had no silver rings in their noses! He crossed Styford bridge without stopping to look over the parapet at the little fishes, swimming head up stream, balanced in the sluggish current; or the white ducks that dabbled amongst floating masses of water-crowsfoot. At Styford Mill he called to leave a message from Aunt Dorcas to the Miller about meal; the Miller's wife gave him an apple.

离磨坊不远有座房子，房子里住着一条大狗，大狗吉普赛成天"汪汪"地叫，但对鲁滨逊却是笑容满面，还摇着尾巴。几辆马车追上了鲁滨逊。开始是两个老农眯着眼睛打量着鲁滨逊，他们有两只鹅、一袋土豆和一些圆白菜，放在两轮马车的后座。后来，一个赶着驴车的老太太路过，车上有七只母鸡，还有长捆的粉色食用大黄，它生长在苹果汁桶下的稻草里。接着，鲁滨逊的表兄小汤姆·皮格走来了，他赶着一辆草莓色沙毛矮种马拉的送奶车，车上的空罐头筒在丁当作响。

At the house beyond the mill, there is a big dog that barks; but the big dog Gypsy only smiled and wagged his tail at Robinson. Several carts and gigs overtook him. First, two old farmers who screwed themselves round to stare at Robinson. They had two geese, a sack of potatoes, and some cabbages, sitting on the back seat of their gig. Then an old woman passed in a donkey cart with seven hens, and long pink bundles of rhubarb that had been grown in straw under apple barrels. Then with a rattle and a jingle of cans came Robinson's cousin, little Tom Pigg, driving a strawberry roan pony, in a milk float.

他碰巧去相反的方向，否则他可能会让鲁滨逊搭车。实际上，那匹草莓色沙毛矮种马正想离家出逃。

"这只小猪去集市！"小汤姆·皮格欢快地喊着，他和"咯吱咯吱"的马车消失在一片尘土中。鲁滨逊被甩在后面，独自站立在小路上。

He might have offered Robinson a lift, only he happened to be going in the opposite direction; in fact, the strawberry roan pony was running away home.

"This little pig went to market!" shouted little Tom Pigg gaily, as he rattled out of sight in a cloud of dust, leaving Robinson standing in the road.

鲁滨逊继续沿着小路往前走,不一会儿,来到对面的篱笆围栏处,小道从这里又沿着田边向前延伸。鲁滨逊把篮子推过围栏,第一次觉得有点害怕。在这块地里,有奶牛、皮毛柔滑发亮的大德文牛,它们的皮肤是深红色的,就像当地土壤的颜色。牛群的首领是一头凶恶的老奶牛,她的角尖上都拴着黄铜球。她很不友善地盯着鲁滨逊。鲁滨逊紧张地穿过草坪,快步地从更远处的梯子走过去。这里是新踩出来的小道,他沿着新一茬青小麦庄稼地边绕过去。有人"砰"地放了一枪,鲁滨逊吓得跳了起来,摔碎了篮里多克斯姨

Robinson walked on along the road, and presently he came to another stile in the opposite hedge, where the footpath followed the fields again. Robinson got his basket through the stile. For the first time he felt some apprehension. In this field there were cows; big sleek Devon cattle, dark red like their native soil. The leader of the herd was a vicious old cow, with brass balls screwed on to the tips of her horns. She stared disagreeably at Robinson. He sidled across the meadow and got out through the farther stile as quickly as he could. Here the new trodden footpath followed round the edge of a crop of young green wheat. Someone let off a gun with a bang that made Robinson jump and cracked one of Aunt Dorcas's

妈的一个鸡蛋。

一大群白嘴鸦和寒鸦从麦地里飞起来,"呱呱"地叫嚷着。从田野边的榆树林传过来火车头的鸣笛声、火车货运车皮调轨的撞击声、车间的噪音、远处城镇的嘈杂声、进港轮船的汽笛声和天空中海鸥嘶哑的叫声,各种各样的声音混杂在一起冲击着小猪鲁滨逊的耳膜。就在此时,斯蒂茅斯镇出现在眼前。

鲁滨逊最后离开了田野,同一群步行和搭乘马车的乡下人一起赶往斯蒂茅斯集市。

eggs in the basket.

A cloud of rooks and jackdaws rose cawing and scolding from the wheat. Other sounds mingled with their cries; noises of the town of Stymouth that began to come in sight through the elm trees that bordered the fields; distant noises from the station; whistling of an engine; the bump of trucks shunting; noise of workshops; the hum of a distant town; the hooter of a steamer entering the harbour. High overhead came the hoarse cry of the gulls, and the squabbling cawing of rooks, old and young, in their rookery up in the elm trees.

Robinson left the fields for the last time and joined a stream of country people on foot and in carts, all going to Stymouth Market.

第四章

斯蒂茅斯是一座美丽的小镇，位于皮格斯戴河的河口，缓慢的河水徐徐地流入海湾。地处山丘盆地中的小镇好像在向下滑动，向着海的方向滑入斯蒂茅斯港，码头和外防洪堤成了港口的屏障。

城镇郊外不太整洁，海港通常也是如此。在西边闭塞的郊区，居住的主要是山羊和那些买卖旧铁制品、破布、焦油粗绳和渔网的人。那里有制绳工厂，洗好的衣物搭在绳子上，在细石海滩的支架

Chapter Four

Stymouth is a pretty little town, situated at the mouth of the river Pigsty, whose sluggish waters slide gently into a bay sheltered by high red headlands. The town itself seems to be sliding downhill in a basin of hills, all slipping seaward into Stymouth harbour, which is dammed back by quays and the outer breakwater.

The outskirts of the town are untidy, as is frequently the case with seaports. A straggling suburb on the western approach is inhabited principally by goats, and persons who deal in old iron, rags, tarred rope, and fishing nets. There are rope walks,

上摇摆着。海草、海螺壳和死螃蟹凌乱地散落在地上。这和波克斯姨妈在干净的绿草地上挂的一排排衣服简直太不一样了。

and washing that flaps on waggling lines above banks of stony shingle, littered with seaweed, whelk shells and dead crabs — very different from Aunt Porcas's clothes lines over the clean green grass.

海上用品商店销售小型望远镜、长雨衣、防水帽和洋葱;各种各样的气味弥漫在空气中;在怪异、高大、岗亭式的建筑里,人们晾晒他们的渔网,大声的谈话声从肮脏的房子里传出来,这些建筑看来适合做仓库。鲁滨逊一直在小路中间走,有人从酒店窗户里朝他叫:"进来,胖猪!"鲁滨逊拔腿就跑。

斯蒂茅斯镇内干净、舒适、风景如画,一切都井然有序(港口总是另一番景象)。但道路向下倾斜,坡度极大,如果鲁滨逊让多克斯姨妈的鸡蛋从市镇商业区大街开始滚,它就会一直滚到底,只是

And there are marine stores that sell spy-glasses, and sou'westers, and onions; and there are smells; and curious high sheds, shaped like sentry boxes, where they hang up herring nets to dry; and loud talking inside dirty houses. It seemed a likely place to meet a pantechnicon. Robinson kept in the middle of the road. Somebody in a public-house shouted at him through the window, "Come in, fat pig!" Robinson took to his heels.

The town of Stymouth itself is clean, pleasant, picturesque, and well-behaved (always excepting the harbour); but it is extremely steep downhill. If Robinson had started one of Aunt Dorcas's eggs rolling at the top of High Street, it would have

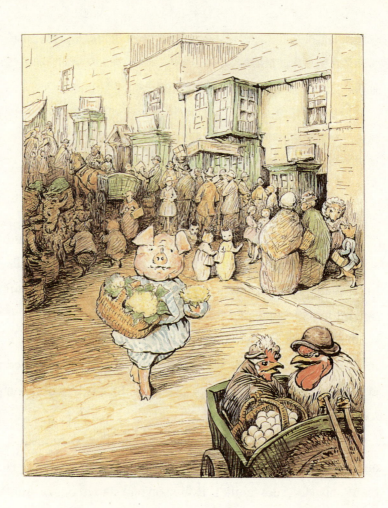

鸡蛋肯定会被门槛挡住碰碎，或者被人踩碎。今天是赶集日，大街上人山人海。

这里道路拥挤，人们行走困难，很难不被人从人行道上挤下来。鲁滨逊遇到的每位老太太，似乎都挎着一只和他一样大的篮子。道路上停放着卖鱼的手推车、卖苹果的手推车、卖陶器和五金制品的摊位，还有矮腿马车上的母鸡，驴背上驮着挂篓，农夫四轮马车上满载干草，还有一长排煤车从码头源源不断地驶过来。对一只乡下的猪来说，噪声都把他弄糊涂了，使他胆战心惊。

rolled all the way down to the bottom; only it would have got broken certainly against a doorstep, or underfoot. There were crowds in the streets, as it was market day.

Indeed, it was difficult to walk about without being pushed off the pavement; every old woman that Robinson met seemed to have a basket as big as his own. In the roadway were fish barrows, apple barrows, stalls with crockery and hardware, cocks and hens riding in pony carts, donkeys with panniers, and farmers with wagon-loads of hay. Also there was a constant string of coal carts coming up from the docks. To a country-bred pig, the noise was confusing and fearful.

一进入福尔大街,鲁滨逊的脑袋就开始"嗡嗡"作响。在大街上,牛贩子养的狗正设法把三头小公牛赶进牛栏,斯达姆比和镇里近一半的狗都来帮忙,顿时乱成一团。鲁滨逊和另外两只小猪拿着芦笋冲进一条小巷,躲在一个门口,一直等到吼声和狗吠声消失。

鲁滨逊鼓起勇气走出来,回到福尔大街,他决定紧跟在驴子后面走,驴子的驮篓里垛着高高的春甘蓝,这样找到去集市的路就没有困难了。但是,耽误了这么长时间之后,教堂的钟已经敲响了11下,当然,这也没什么可奇怪的了。

Robinson kept his head very creditably until he got into Fore Street, where a drover's dog was trying to turn three bullocks into a yard, assisted by Stumpy and half the other dogs of the town. Robinson and two other little pigs with baskets of asparagus bolted down an alley and hid in a doorway until the noise of bellowing and barking had passed.

When Robinson took courage to come out again into Fore Street, he decided to follow close behind the tail of a donkey who was carrying panniers piled high with spring broccoli. There was no difficulty in guessing which road led to market. But after all these delays it was not surprising that the church clock struck eleven.

尽管集市十点钟就开门了,可是许多顾客仍在集市大厅里购物,而且后边还有人不断地进来。大厅是一个宽敞的、通风的、明亮的、使人愉快的地方,顶篷是玻璃的。与在外面鹅卵石大街上的推撞和吵闹相比,尽管这里也很拥挤,但是却安全、使人高兴。无论如何,那儿没有被车轧着的危险。嘈杂的嗡嗡声在大厅里回荡,卖货人大声叫卖,顾客在货摊周围拥挤,支架木板上展示着各色奶制品、蔬菜、鱼和甲壳类动物。

在南尼·内蒂戈特卖海螺的摊位的另一端,鲁滨逊找到了一个可以站着的空位。

Although it had been open since ten, there were still plenty of customers buying, and wanting to buy, in the market hall. It was a large, airy, light, cheerful, covered-in place, with glass in the roof. It was crowded, but safe and pleasant, compared with the jostling and racket outside in the cobble-paved streets; at all events there was no risk of being run over. There was a loud hum of voices; market folk cried their wares; customers elbowed and pushed round the stalls. Dairy produce, vegetables, fish, and shell fish were displayed upon the flat boards on trestles.

Robinson had found a standing place at one end of a stall where Nanny Nettigoat was selling periwinkles.

"海螺、海螺！啰、啰、啰！咩，咩，咩！"南尼吆喝着。

她专卖海螺，所以对鲁滨逊卖的鸡蛋和樱草花毫不嫉妒，对鲁滨逊卖的菜花更是一无所知。鲁滨逊有意把菜花放在桌下的篮子里，站在支架台后的空箱上，雄赳赳气昂昂地吆喝道：

"鸡蛋，刚下的！刚下的鲜鸡蛋！谁来买我的鸡蛋和黄水仙花？"

"我买，肯定买，我要一打。罗斯小姐派我来集市，就是要买鸡蛋和黄油的。"一条尾巴短粗的大黄狗说。

"Winkle, winkle! Wink, wink, wink! Maa, maa-a!" bleated Nanny.

Winkles were the only thing that she offered for sale, so she felt no jealousy of Robinson's eggs and primroses. She knew nothing about his cauliflowers; he had the sense to keep them in the basket under the table. He stood on an empty box, quite proud and bold behind the trestle table, singing:

"Eggs, new laid! Fresh new-laid eggs! Who'll come and buy my eggs and daffodillies?"

"I will, sure," said a large brown dog with a stumpy tail, "I'll buy a dozen. My Miss Rose has sent me to market on purpose to buy eggs and butter."

"很抱歉,我没有黄油,斯达姆比先生,但是我有漂亮的菜花。"鲁滨逊说着小心地看了一眼南尼·内蒂戈特,担心她把菜花吃了,然后提起篮子让斯达姆比看,南尼这时候正忙着给戴苏格兰便帽的鸭顾客量海螺。"除了一个碎鸡蛋,全是可爱的浅黄色鸡蛋。我想,对面货摊的那只白猫咪在卖黄油——多好的菜花呀,快来买呀!"

"我要买一棵菜花,亲爱的,保佑他的小翘鼻子。是你自己菜园子里种的吗?"老贝齐匆忙地走过来。她的风湿病好了一些,出门时已把家托付给苏珊了。"不,亲爱的,我不要鸡蛋,我自己养

"I am so sorry, I have no butter, Mr. Stumpy; but I have beautiful cauliflowers," said Robinson, lifting up the basket, after a cautious glance round at Nanny Nettigoat, who might have tried to nibble them. She was busy measuring periwinkles in a pewter mug for a duck customer in a tam-o'-shanter cap. "They are lovely brown eggs, except one that got cracked; I think that white pussy cat at the opposite stall is selling butter — they are beautiful cauliflowers."

"I'll buy a cauliflower, lovey, bless his little turned-up nose; did he grow them in his own garden?" said old Betsy, bustling up; her rheumatism was better; she had left Susan to keep house. "No, lovey, I don't want any eggs; I keep hens

鸡。请你给我一棵菜花，和一把插花瓶的黄水仙花。"贝齐说。

"噢，噢，噢！"鲁滨逊回答说。

"这儿，珀金斯太太，到这儿来！你瞧，这只小猪自己一人站在货摊边！"

"哎呀，我可不知道！"珀金斯太太大声地说，从人群中挤了过去，后面跟着两个小女孩。"哎，我想知道！孩子，这是新下的鸡蛋吗？不会像怀恩多特太太的鸡蛋那样，'啪'的一声炸开，把我最好的衣服弄脏吧？怀恩多特太太的鸡蛋在第五届花卉展览会上得了第一名，但好景不长，后来鸡蛋爆炸了，把裁判员的黑丝长袍弄脏

myself. A cauliflower and a bunch of daffodils for a bow-pot, please," said Betsy.

"Wee, wee, wee!" replied Robinson.

"Here, Mrs. Perkins, come here! Look at this little pig stuck up at a stall all by himself!"

"Well, I don't know!" exclaimed Mrs. Perkins, pushing through the crowd, followed by two little girls. "Well, I never! Are they quite new laid, sonny? Won't go off pop and spoil my Sunday dress like the eggs Mrs. Wyandotte took first prize with at five flower shows, till they popped and spoiled the

了。不会是鸭蛋、用咖啡染过的吧?这是花展的骗人把戏!刚下的蛋,敢担保吗?你说只有一个碎了?我认为你说的是老实话。碎蛋炸起来吃并不坏,请给我一打鸡蛋和一棵菜花。瞧,萨拉·波利!瞧他的鼻环。"

　　萨拉·波利和她的年轻女友突然咯咯大笑起来,弄得鲁滨逊脸都红了。他非常尴尬,要不是一位女士碰了他一下,他甚至都没有注意到她想买菜花。除了一把樱草花,没有别的可卖了。两个小女孩"咯咯"地笑着,交头接耳了一番,就回来买了那把樱草花,她

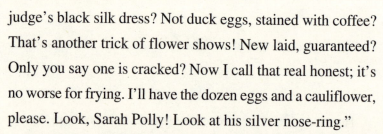

judge's black silk dress? Not duck eggs, stained with coffee? That's another trick of flower shows! New laid, guaranteed? Only you say one is cracked? Now I call that real honest; it's no worse for frying. I'll have the dozen eggs and a cauliflower, please. Look, Sarah Polly! Look at his silver nose-ring."

　　Sarah Polly and her little girl friend went into fits of giggling, so that Robinson blushed. He was so confused that he did not notice a lady who wanted to buy his last cauliflower, till she touched him. There was nothing else left to sell, but a bunch of primroses. After more giggling and some whispering the two little girls came back, and bought the primroses. They

们给了他一块薄荷糖和一个便士。鲁滨逊接过来,但没有表现出太大的热情,而是若有所思的样子。

麻烦就出在他刚卖掉那把樱草花,就发现他把波克斯姨妈给他做样子用的织补毛线也一起卖掉了。他不知道是不是应该要回来,可是珀金斯太太、萨拉·波利和她的年轻女友都不见了。

鲁滨逊卖完东西,从集市大厅出来,嘴里含着薄荷糖,这时还不断有人到大厅来。鲁滨逊出门下台阶的时候,篮子挂住了挤上来

gave him a peppermint, as well as the penny, which Robinson accepted; but without enthusiasm and with a preoccupied manner.

The trouble was that no sooner had he parted with the bunch of primroses than he realised that he had also sold Aunt Porcas's pattern of darning wool. He wondered if he ought to ask for it back; but Mrs. Perkins and Sarah Polly and her little girl friend had disappeared.

Robinson, having sold everything, came out of the market hall, sucking the peppermint. There were still numbers of people coming in. As Robinson came out upon the steps his

的老母羊的披肩。就在这时候,斯达姆比出来了。斯达姆比做完了买卖,篮子里面装满了采购的物品,沉甸甸的。他是一只有责任心、值得信赖、体贴人的狗,总是愿意帮助别人。

鲁滨逊问他去芒比先生家怎么走,斯达姆比说:"我回家就经过布罗德大街。跟我走吧,我会告诉你的。"

"噢,噢,噢!哎呀,谢谢你,斯达姆比!"鲁滨逊说。

basket got caught in the shawl of an elderly sheep, who was pushing her way up. While Robinson was disentangling it, Stumpy came out. He had finished his marketing. His basket was full of heavy purchases. A responsible, trustworthy, obliging dog was Stumpy, glad to do a kindness to anybody.

When Robinson asked him the way to Mr. Mumby's, Stumpy said: "I am going home by Broad Street. Come with me, and I will show you."

"Wee, wee, wee! Oh, thank you, Stumpy!" said Robinson.

第五章

老芒比先生是一位戴眼镜的聋老头儿,经营一家百货店。除了火腿,他几乎卖你能想到的所有东西——多克斯姨妈十分赞许这种经营方式,它是斯蒂茅斯惟一的一家百货店,在柜台上你看不到大盘里一串串让人看了生厌的细长灰暗的生香肠,也没有从天花板上挂下来的卷熏肉。

Chapter Five

Old Mr. Mumby was a deaf old man in spectacles, who kept a general store. He sold almost anything you can imagine, except ham — a circumstance much approved by Aunt Dorcas. It was the only general store in Stymouth where you would not find displayed upon the counter a large dish, containing strings of thin, pale-coloured, repulsively uncooked sausages, and rolled bacon hanging from the ceiling.

多克斯姨妈深有感触地说:"有什么乐趣?当你一走进店铺,脑袋就碰上一只火腿,你会有什么乐趣呢?那火腿可能就是你远房表兄弟的腿。"

"What pleasure," said Aunt Dorcas feelingly — "what possible pleasure can there be in entering a shop where you knock your head against a ham? A ham that may have belonged to a dear second cousin?"

因此，鲁滨逊的姨妈都是从老芒比先生那儿买糖、茶叶、蓝纸袋、肥皂、长柄平底锅、火柴和大杯子。

他卖的所有东西，还有许多其他的东西，如果没有库存，他就会根据定单去提货。但是，酵母得需要很新鲜的，所以他不卖；他建议鲁滨逊到一家面包店去要一点；还说，现在买圆白菜种子，已经过了季节，今年所有的人都已经播下了圆白菜种子。他卖过织补的精纺毛线，但是，鲁滨逊已经忘记要买哪种颜色的了。

Therefore the aunts bought their sugar and tea, their blue bag, their soap, their frying pans, matches, and mugs from old Mr. Mumby.

All these things he sold, and many more besides, and what he did not keep in stock he would obtain to order. But yeast requires to be quite fresh, he did not sell it; he advised Robinson to ask for yeast at a baker's shop. Also he said it was too late in the season to buy cabbage seed; everybody had finished sowing vegetable seeds this year. Worsted for darning he did sell; but Robinson had forgotten the colour.

鲁滨逊用他的便士买了六根叫人喜欢的黏麦芽糖，还仔细地听芒比先生给多克斯姨妈和波克斯姨妈带回的口信——等驴车修好以后，下个星期他们将送过去一些圆白菜；水壶至今还没有修好的原因；他愿意向波克斯姨妈推荐一种新获专利的熨斗。

鲁滨逊一边说"噢，噢，噢？"一边专心地听着。小狗蒂普金斯站在柜台后的凳子上，把装着杂货的蓝纸袋的袋口系上，然后低声地问鲁滨逊："今年春天在皮戈瑞·波康比的粮仓里有老鼠吗？鲁滨逊星期六下午将做些什么？"

Robinson bought six sticks of delightfully sticky barley sugar with his pennies, and listened carefully to Mr. Mumby's messages for Aunt Dorcas and Aunt Porcas — how they were to send some cabbages next week when the donkey cart would be mended; and how the kettle was not repaired yet, and there was a new patent box-iron he would like to recommend to Aunt Porcas.

Robinson said "Wee, wee, wee?" and listened, and little dog Tipkins who stood on a stool behind the counter, tying up grocery parcels in blue paper bags — little dog Tipkins whispered to Robinson — "Were there any rats this spring in the barn at Piggery Porcombe? And what would Robinson be doing on Saturday afternoon?"

"噢，噢，噢！"鲁滨逊回答。

鲁滨逊从芒比先生的杂货店出来，挎着沉沉的东西。虽然麦芽糖让人很开心，但是他仍然为没有买到织补毛线、酵母和圆白菜种子而感到不安。他焦急地四处张望，突然他又碰到了贝齐。贝齐大声地说：

"上帝保佑这只小猪！怎么还没有回家？这个时候在斯蒂茅斯千万不要停留，否则会遇到小偷的！"

鲁滨逊说出了他丢失织补毛线的事，感到很为难。

和蔼的老贝齐准备帮助他。

"Wee, wee, wee!" answered Robinson.

Robinson came out of Mr. Mumby's, heavily laden. The barley sugar was comforting; but he was troubled about the darning wool, the yeast, and the cabbage seed. He was looking about rather anxiously, when again he met old Betsy, who exclaimed:

"Bless the little piggy! Not gone home yet? Now it must not stop in Stymouth till it gets its pocket picked!"

Robinson explained his difficulty about the darning wool.

Kind old Betsy was ready with help.

小猪鲁滨逊的故事
The Tale of Little Pig Robinson

"哎呀,我注意到那段毛线系在樱草花束上了,毛线是蓝灰色的,就像我给萨姆最近织的那双短袜子的颜色。跟我来,咱们去毛线店 —— 弗利西·弗洛克的毛线店,我记得那个颜色,是的,我记得很清楚!"贝齐说。

弗洛克太太就是遇到鲁滨逊的那只羊,她买了三个萝卜,就从集市直接回家了,因为她怕商店上了锁会失去顾客。

这样的商店!这么杂乱!各种颜色的毛线,粗毛线、细毛线、手织用的毛线、编织地毯的毛线,成捆成捆地混杂在一起。她什么

"Why, I noticed the wool round the little primrose posy; it was blue-grey colour like the last pair of socks that I knitted for Sam. Come with me to the wool shop — Fleecy Flock's wool shop. I remember the colour; well I do!" said Betsy.

Mrs. Flock was the sheep that had run against Robinson; she had bought herself three turnips and come straight home from market, for fear of missing customers while her shop was locked up.

Such a shop! Such a jumble! Wool all sorts of colours, thick wool, thin wool, fingering wool, and rug wool, bundles and bundles all jumbled up; and she could not put her hoof on anything. She was so confused and slow at finding things that

东西都找不到,又糊涂,动作又慢,贝齐不耐烦了。

"不是,我不是要织拖鞋的毛线,是织补毛线,弗利西。织补毛线,和我买来给萨姆织毛袜子的一样颜色。天呀,不是,不是织毛线针!是织补毛线。"

"巴巴,巴巴!夫人,你说是白色的还是黑色的?三股线的,是吗?"

"哟,哎呀,是蓝灰色织补毛线,不是杂色的。"

"我原来知道在哪儿有。"弗利西·弗洛克无奈地说,把线捆全翻乱了。"西姆·拉姆今天早上带来一些尤汉普顿首饰别针,把我的

Betsy got impatient.

"No, I don't want wool for slippers; *darning wool*, Fleecy; darning wool, same colour as I bought for my Sam's socks. Bless me, *no*, not knitting needles! Darning wool."

"Baa, baa! Did you say white or black, m'm? Three ply, was it?"

"Oh, dear me, *grey* darning wool on cards; not heather mixture."

"I know I have it somewhere," said Fleecy Flock helplessly, jumbling up the skeins and bundles. "Sim Ram came in this morning with part of the Ewehampton clip; my shop is

商店全塞满了!"

弗利西用了半个小时才找到那种毛线,要不是贝齐和他一起去,鲁滨逊绝不可能买到毛线。

"这么晚了,我该回家了。"贝齐说,"我的萨姆今天上岸吃晚饭。如果你听我的话,你先把这么重的大篮子寄放在戈尔芬奇斯小姐那里,赶紧把该买的东西买了,回皮戈瑞·波康比的家要走很长的一段上坡路呢。"

鲁滨逊急忙按老贝齐说的,去找戈尔芬奇斯小姐。在去的路上,他来到一家面包房,他想起了酵母。

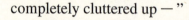

completely cluttered up —"

It took half an hour to find the wool. If Betsy had not been with him, Robinson never would have got it.

"It's that late, I must go home," said Betsy. "My Sam is on shore today for dinner. If you take my advice you will leave that big heavy basket with the Miss Goldfinches, and hurry with your shopping. It's a long uphill walk home to Piggery Porcombe."

Robinson, anxious to follow old Betsy's advice, walked towards the Miss Goldfinches. On the way he came to a baker's, and he remembered the yeast.

遗憾的是，这不是那种正宗的面包房。一股好香的烤面包味扑鼻而来，橱窗里陈列着糕点，不过，这是一家餐饮店或小饭馆。

他推开旋转门，一位穿围裙、头戴方形白帽的男人转过身来，对他说："你好！这个猪肉馅饼是用后腿走进来的吗？"坐在饭桌旁的四个粗汉子大笑起来。

鲁滨逊急忙离开了那个商店，不敢再去任何一家面包房了。他苦闷地朝福尔大街的另一个窗户看去，突然斯达姆比又看见他了。斯达姆比已经把他自己的篮子送回家了，正出来要办另一件事。他

It was not the right sort of baker's, unfortunately. There was a nice bakery smell, and pastry in the window; but it was an eating house or cook shop.

When he pushed the swing door open, a man in an apron and a square white cap turned round and said, "Hullo! Is this a pork pie walking on its hind legs?" — and four rude men at a dining table burst out laughing.

Robinson left the shop in a hurry. He felt afraid to go into any other baker's shop. He was looking wistfully into another window in Fore Street when Stumpy saw him again. He had taken his own basket home, and come out on another errand.

嘴里衔着鲁滨逊的篮子,带他去了一家非常可靠的面包房。他经常到这里给自己买狗饼干,鲁滨逊终于给多克斯姨妈买到了酵母。

他们没能买到圆白菜种子,听说惟一可能买到的地方,是在码头一家由一对鹡鸰鸟经营的小商店。

"可惜我不能跟你一起去,"斯达姆比说,"我的罗斯小姐扭伤了脚脖子,她派我来买12张邮票,我必须在邮件发出以前拿回家给她。不要拿这么重的篮子上下台阶,把它留给戈尔芬奇斯小姐好了。"

He carried Robinson's basket in his mouth and took him to a very safe baker's, where he was accustomed to buy dog biscuits for himself. There Robinson purchased Aunt Dorcas's yeast at last.

They searched in vain for cabbage seed; they were told that the only likely place was a little store on the quay, kept by a pair of wagtails.

"It is a pity I cannot go with you," said Stumpy. "My Miss Rose has sprained her ankle; she sent me to fetch twelve postage stamps, and I must take them home to her, before the post goes out. Do not try to carry this heavy basket down and up the steps; leave it with the Miss Goldfinches."

鲁滨逊非常感激斯达姆比。戈尔芬奇斯家的两位小姐经营着一家有茶和咖啡的旅店,是多克斯姨妈和一些喜欢安静的赶集人经常光顾的地方。店门上挂了一块招牌,上面画了一只叫作"满足的西丝金"的小胖绿鸟,这就是旅店的招牌。店里还设有马厩,每星期六搬运工的驴子把洗好的衣物驮到斯蒂茅斯来,驴子就在那里休息。

鲁滨逊看上去非常劳累,年长一些的戈尔芬奇斯小姐递给他一杯茶。她们俩都不约而同地要他立刻把茶喝掉。

"噢,噢,噢!哟克,哟克!"鲁滨逊喊着,茶水的热气烫着了他的鼻子。

Robinson was very grateful to Stumpy. The two Miss Goldfinches kept a tea and coffee tavern which was patronized by Aunt Dorcas and the quieter market people. Over the door was a sign board upon which was painted a fat little green bird called "The Contented Siskin", which was the name of their coffee tavern. They had a stable where the carrier's donkey rested when it came into Stymouth with the washing on Saturdays.

Robinson looked so tired that the elder Miss Goldfinch gave him a cup of tea; but they both told him to drink it up quickly.

"Wee, wee, wee! Yock yock!" said Robinson, scalding his nose.

尽管她们都尊重多克斯姨妈,但戈尔芬奇斯家的两位小姐都不赞成让鲁滨逊独自出来买东西,那个篮子对他来说太重了。

"我们谁也提不起这个篮子。"那位年长一些的戈尔芬奇斯小姐说着,伸出一只小爪子,"快去买你的圆白菜种子,买完就赶快回家吧。西姆·拉姆的马车还在我们的马厩里等着呢。如果你能在他出发之前回来,我肯定他会让你搭车的。无论如何,他会在他的座位底下腾出一块地方放你的篮子——他会经过皮戈瑞·波康比。快跑吧!"

"噢,噢,噢!"鲁滨逊说。

In spite of their respect for Aunt Dorcas, the Miss Goldfinches disapproved of his solitary shopping; and they said that the basket was far too heavy for him.

"Neither of us could lift it," said the elder Miss Goldfinch, holding out a tiny claw. "Get your cabbage seed and hurry back. Sim Ram's pony gig is still waiting in our stable. If you come back before he starts I feel sure he will give you a lift; at all events he will make room for your basket under the seat — and he passes Piggery Porcombe. Run away now!"

"Wee, wee, wee!" said Robinson.

"她们究竟是怎么想的,会让他自己出来?天黑前他绝对到不了家。"那位年长的戈尔芬奇斯小姐说,"克拉拉,飞到马厩去,告诉西姆·拉姆的矮脚马,鲁滨逊篮子没有放上马车以前不要走。"

年轻的戈尔芬奇斯小姐飞过院子,她们是勤劳活泼的小瓢虫。她们把方糖、蓟花种子和茶叶放在茶叶罐里。她们的桌子和瓷器都一尘不染。

"Whatever were they thinking of to let him come alone? He will never get home before dark," said the elder Miss Goldfinch. "Fly to the stable, Clara; tell Sim Ram's pony not to start without the basket."

The younger Miss Goldfinch flew across the yard. They were industrious, sprightly little lady birds, who kept lump sugar and thistle seed as well as tea in their tea-caddies. Their tables and china were spotlessly clean.

第六章

斯蒂茅斯到处都是酒店和旅店,简直是太多了。农夫通常把马放在"布莱克·布尔"或者"霍斯和法里尔"马厩,集市小贩则喜欢住在"皮格和惠斯"旅店里。

一个叫"克朗和安克尔"的小旅店坐落在福尔大街的拐角上,这是水手们常去的地方。有几个水手,手插在兜里,在店门周围闲逛,一个身穿蓝运动服的水手穿过街去,两眼紧盯着鲁滨逊。

Chapter Six

Stymouth was full of inns; too full. The farmers usually put up their horses at the "Black Bull" or the "Horse and Farrier"; the smaller market people patronized the "Pig and Whistle".

There was another inn called the "Crown and Anchor" at the corner of Fore Street. It was much frequented by seamen; several were lounging about the door with their hands in their pockets. One sailor-man in a blue jersey sauntered across the road, staring very hard at Robinson.

他说："我说，小猪！你喜欢鼻烟吗？"

现在，如果说鲁滨逊有什么不对之处，那就是他不会说"不"，甚至对一个偷鸡蛋的刺猬也不会说。事实上，鼻烟或烟草使他难受。但他没有说"不要，谢谢，曼先生"，然后调头去干他自己的事，而是拖着双脚，眼睛半闭，头歪到一侧，"哼哼"地叫。

水手掏出一个角质鼻烟盒，送了一点鼻烟给鲁滨逊。鲁滨逊用一块小纸把它包了起来，打算送给多克斯姨妈。为了不失礼，他送给水手一些麦芽糖。

Said he — "I say, little pig! do you like snuff?"

Now if Robinson had a fault, it was that he could not say "No"; not even to a hedgehog stealing eggs. As a matter of fact, snuff or tobacco made him sick. But instead of saying, "No, thank you, Mr. Man," and going straight away about his business, he shuffled his feet, half closed one eye, hung his head on one side, and grunted.

The sailor pulled out a horn snuff box and presented a small pinch to Robinson, who wrapped it up in a little bit of paper, intending to give it to Aunt Dorcas. Then, not to be outdone in politeness, he offered the sailor-man some barley sugar.

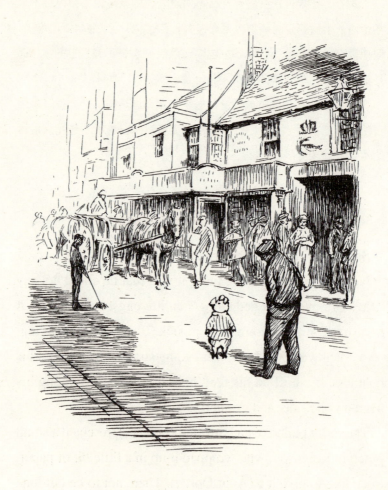

虽然鲁滨逊不喜欢鼻烟,但是,他的新朋友却不反对吃糖,而且吃了很多。他揪了揪鲁滨逊的耳朵,并向他致意,还说他有五层下巴。他答应带鲁滨逊去卖圆白菜种子的商店,最后,还希望能有幸带鲁滨逊去参观一艘贩卖生姜的商船,船名叫"坎德尔斯的庞德",船长是巴纳巴斯·布彻。

鲁滨逊不喜欢那个名字,这使他想起油脂、猪油、烤熏肉炉中发出的干柴燃烧的"噼啪"声和熏肉配菜。但他还是跟着走了,脸上还带着羞涩的笑容,小心地用脚尖着地。可是鲁滨逊不知道,那个人就是船上的厨师!

If Robinson was not fond of snuff, at all events his new acquaintance had no objection to candy. He ate an alarming quantity. Then he pulled Robinson's ear and complimented him, and said he had five chins. He promised to take Robinson to the cabbage seed shop;and, finally, he begged to have the honour of showing him over a ship engaged in the ginger trade, commanded by Captain Barnabas Butcher, and named the "Pound of Candles".

Robinson did not very much like the name. It reminded him of tallow, of lard, of crackle and trimmings of bacon. But he allowed himself to be led away, smiling shyly, and walking on his toes. If Robinson had only known . . . that man was a ship's cook!

当他们从海伊大街拐进一条又陡又窄的巷子、向海港走的时候,老芒比先生在他的商店门口焦急地喊:"鲁滨逊!鲁滨逊!"但是因为过往马车的噪声太大,鲁滨逊没有听见。这时正好又有顾客进来,分散了芒比的注意力,使芒比忘了水手可疑的举动。否则,他会毫不犹豫地命令他的狗蒂普金斯去把鲁滨逊找回来。实际上,当鲁滨逊失踪以后,第一个向警察提供有用信息的就是他,但那时已经太晚了。

As they turned down the steep narrow lane, out of High Street, leading to the harbour, old Mr. Mumby at his shop door called out anxiously, "Robinson! Robinson!" But there was too much noise of carts. And a customer coming into the shop at that moment distracted his attention, and he forgot the suspicious behaviour of the sailor. Otherwise, out of regard to the family, he would undoubtedly have ordered his dog, Tipkins, to go and fetch Robinson back. As it was, he was the first person to give useful information to the police, when Robinson had been missed. But it was then too late.

鲁滨逊和他的新朋友走下很长一段台阶，来到港口的船坞——台阶非常高，而且又陡又滑。小猪只得一级一级地蹦，直到水手十分善意地拉住他。他们手拉手地沿着码头走，看上去非常开心。

鲁滨逊饶有兴趣地向他周围观看。当初来到斯蒂茅斯的时候，他在驴车上曾瞥见过那些台阶，但是决不敢冒险从台阶上下来，因为水手相当粗鲁，而且他们经常让狂吠的猎狗看守他们的船只。

海港停泊着许多船只。这里的噪声和镇里面的集市广场几乎没

Robinson and his new friend went down the long flight of steps to the harbour basin — very high steps, steep and slippery. The little pig was obliged to jump from step to step until the sailor kindly took hold of him. They walked along the quay hand in hand; their appearance seemed to cause unbounded amusement.

Robinson looked about him with much interest. He had peeped over those steps before when he had come into Stymouth in the donkey cart, but he had never ventured to go down, because the sailors are rather rough, and because they frequently have little snarling terriers on guard about their vessels.

There were ever so many ships in the harbour; the noise and bustle was almost as loud as it had been up above in the

有区别。一艘名叫"戈尔迪洛克斯"的三桅大帆船正在卸下一批橙子。码头更远的泊位上停靠着一艘双桅横帆的"利特尔·博·皮普"号,成捆的来自尤汉普顿和拉姆沃西的羊毛正被装上船。

长着弯犄角、系着铃铛的老西姆·拉姆正站在舷门旁统计数字。每次吊车旋转过来,通过滑轮迅速下滑的绳索卸下一捆羊毛,西姆·拉姆就点一下头,铃铛也随着"丁丁冬冬"地响起来,他还发出粗哑的"咩咩"声。

拉姆一眼就认出了鲁滨逊,他曾经赶着马车路过皮戈瑞·波康

market square. A big three-masted ship called the "Goldielocks" was discharging a cargo of oranges; and farther along the quay, a small coasting brig called "Little Bo Peep" of Bristol was loading up with bales of wool belonging to the sheep of Ewehampton and Lambworthy.

Old Sim Ram, with a sheepbell and big curly horns, stood by the gangway keeping count of the bales. Every time the crane swung round and let down another bale of wool into the hold, with a scuffle of rope through the pulley, Simon Ram nodded his old head, and the bell went "tinkle tinkle, tong", and he gave a gruff bleat.

He was a person who knew Robinson by sight and ought to have warned him. He had often passed Piggery Porcombe

比，他本来应该提醒他的。但他那只失明的眼睛却转向了码头。他刚刚和船上的事务长们吵了一架，因为搞不清楚已吊上船的羊毛，到底是 34 捆还是 35 捆。这使他心烦意乱。

when he drove down the lane in his gig. But his blind eye was turned towards the quay; and he had been flustered and confused by an argument with the pursers as to whether thirty-five bales of wool had been hoisted on board already or only thirty-four.

因此，他把他那只有用的眼睛，小心地盯着那些羊毛，根据木签上的刻痕来计数，一捆一个刻痕——35，36，37。他希望最后统计的数字是对的。

他的短尾牧羊犬，蒂莫西·吉普也认识鲁滨逊，但他当时正忙着监督一场殴斗——运煤船"马杰里·道"号的艾儿代尔猎狗和"戈尔迪洛克斯"号船的西班牙狗之间的一场殴斗正在激烈地进行着。谁都没有注意到他们的狂吠和吼叫，最后他们双双从码头一侧滚下去，掉进水里。鲁滨逊紧跟着水手，牢牢地拉住他的手。

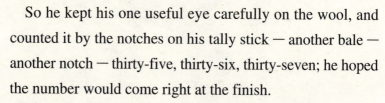

So he kept his one useful eye carefully on the wool, and counted it by the notches on his tally stick — another bale — another notch — thirty-five, thirty-six, thirty-seven; he hoped the number would come right at the finish.

His bob-tailed sheepdog, Timothy Gyp, was also acquainted with Robinson, but he was busy superintending a dog fight between an Airedale terrier belonging to the collier "Margery Dawe" and a Spanish dog belonging to the "Goldielocks". No one took any notice of their growling and snarling, which ended in both rolling over the side of the quay and falling into the water. Robinson kept close to the sailor and held his hand very tight.

"坎德尔斯的庞德"号确实是一艘相当大的帆船,刚刷过油漆,挂着某种标志的旗子,但是鲁滨逊不懂它们的含意。帆船停泊在登岸码头的外端。潮水涨得很快,海浪拍打着船的两侧,码头上固定船的粗缆绳绷得紧紧的。

在船长巴纳巴斯·布彻的指导下,船员们将货物装上船。布彻船长身体瘦长,棕色皮肤,说话声音粗哑,是一位航海家。他做事粗手粗脚的,爱发牢骚,有时候讲话的声音码头上都能听见。这时,他正谈到有关拖船"西-霍斯"——关于春潮和紧接其后刮起的

The "Pound of Candles" proved to be a good-sized schooner, newly painted and decorated with certain flags, whose significance was not understood by Robinson. She lay near the outer end of the jetty. The tide was running up fast, lapping against the ship's sides and straining the thick hawsers by which she was moored to the quay.

The crew were stowing goods on board and doing things with ropes under the direction of Captain Barnabas Butcher; a lean, brown, nautical person with a rasping voice. He banged things about and grumbled; parts of his remarks were audible on the quay. He was speaking about the tug "Sea-horse" — and about the spring tide, with a north-east wind behind it —

东北风,面包店主和蔬菜,11点准时装船,否则……他突然终止了谈话,眼光落在厨师和鲁滨逊身上。

鲁滨逊和厨师从一个摇摇晃晃的木板上上了船。当鲁滨逊登上甲板后,他发现一只大黄猫正站在他对面,给许多黑皮靴上油。

猫吃了一惊,丢下鞋刷子,眨了眨眼,向鲁滨逊做了个鬼脸。鲁滨逊从没见过猫的这种表现,便问猫是不是生病了。厨师向猫扔了一只靴子,猫向上一跳,蹿上了帆索。而鲁滨逊受到最盛情的邀请,到下面船舱里吃松饼和烤面饼。

and the baker's man and fresh vegetables —"to be shipped at eleven sharp; likewise a joint of..." He stopped short suddenly, and his eye lighted upon the cook and Robinson.

Robinson and the cook went on board across a shaky plank. When Robinson stepped on to the deck, he found himself face to face with a large yellow cat who was blacking boots.

The cat gave a start of surprise and dropped its blacking brush. It then began to wink and make extraordinary faces at Robinson. He had never seen a cat behave in that way before. He inquired whether it was ill. Whereupon the cook threw a boot at it, and it rushed up into the rigging. But Robinson he invited most affably to descend into the cabin, to partake of muffins and crumpets.

我不知道鲁滨逊到底吃了多少块松饼。他不停地吃,最后睡着了,一直睡到他的椅子猛晃一下。他从椅子上摔下来,滚到了桌子底下。船舱地板的一侧向天花板摆过去,天花板另一侧又向地板摆回来,碟子满天飞舞。喊叫声、捶击声、链条"咯咯"的撞击声和其他噪音响成一片。

鲁滨逊爬了起来,感到被撞伤了。他从一种梯子式的楼梯爬上甲板,发出阵阵恐惧的尖叫声。船被包围在绿色的巨浪之中,码头上的房子变得像玩具一样小。但在内陆的高处,在红色峭壁和绿色

I do not know how many muffins Robinson consumed. He went on eating them until he fell asleep; and he went on sleeping until his stool gave a lurch, and he fell off and rolled under the table. One side of the cabin floor swung up to the ceiling; and the other side of the ceiling swung down to the floor. Plates danced about; and there were shoutings and thumpings and rattling of chains and other bad sounds.

Robinson picked himself up, feeling bumped. He scrambled up a sort of a ladder-staircase on to the deck. Then he gave squeal upon squeal of horror! All round the ship there were great big green waves; the houses on the quay were like dolls' houses; and high up inland, above the red cliffs and green

田野上，鲁滨逊看见了皮戈瑞·波康比的农场，尽管看上去还不及一张邮票那么大。果园里的一小块白色是波克斯姨妈把洗好的衣物摊在草地上，晾干晒白的地方。在附近，黑色拖船"西－霍斯"号，烟囱冒着青烟，在波浪中前后颠簸，左右摇摆。水手正在把从帆船"坎德尔斯的庞德"号上放下去的缆绳收起来。

船长巴纳巴斯站在帆船的船头上，向拖船船长大声呼喊，水手也向他呼喊。他们一起用力扬起船帆，紧跟上去，迎风搏浪快速前进，大海的气息扑面而来。

至于鲁滨逊——他在甲板上到处乱闯，就像一个神经错乱的

fields, he could see the farm of Piggery Porcombe looking no bigger than a postage stamp. A little white patch in the orchard was Aunt Porcas's washing, spread out to bleach upon the grass. Near at hand the black tug "Sea-horse" smoked and plunged and rolled. They were winding in the tow rope which had just been cast loose from the "Pound of Candles".

Captain Barnabas stood up in the bows of his schooner; he yelled and shouted to the master of the tug. The sailors shouted also, and pulled with a will, and hoisted the sails. The ship heeled over and rushed through the waves, and there was a smell of the sea.

As for Robinson — he tore round and round the deck like

人,大声尖叫。因为甲板倾斜得实在厉害,他滑倒了一两次,可是还跑个不停。他的尖叫声渐渐地平静下来,变成了歌声,但他仍继续在跑。他这样唱道:

"可怜的猪啊,鲁滨逊·克鲁索!

哎呀,他们竟会给他这样的折磨?

把他放在一艘可怕的船上,饱受海浪的颠簸,

哎呀,可怜的猪啊,鲁滨逊·克鲁索!"

one distracted, shrieking very shrill and loud. Once or twice he slipped down; for the deck was extremely sideways; but still he ran and he ran. Gradually his squeals subsided into singing, but still he kept on running, and this is what he sang —

"Poor Pig Robinson Crusoe!

Oh, how in the world could they do so?

They have set him afloat, in a horrible boat,

Oh, poor pig Robinson Crusoe!"

水手们笑得眼泪都流出来了。可是,当鲁滨逊同一段歌词唱了大约五十遍,又在好几个人的腿中间冲来冲去时,就把他们惹急了。水手们开始发脾气了,甚至船上的厨师对他也不客气了,非但不客气,简直是太粗鲁了。他说如果鲁滨逊不停止用他的鼻子唱歌,就把他剁成猪排。

鲁滨逊晕了过去,直挺挺地倒在"坎德尔斯的庞德"号的甲板上。

The sailors laughed until they cried; but when Robinson had sung that same verse about fifty times, and upset several sailors by rushing between their legs, they began to get angry. Even the ship's cook was no longer civil to Robinson. On the contrary, he was very rude indeed. He said that if Robinson did not leave off singing through his nose, he would make him into pork chops.

Then Robinson fainted, and fell flat upon the deck of the "Pound of Candles".

第七章

绝对不要以为鲁滨逊在船上被亏待了,事实恰恰相反,他在"坎德尔斯的庞德"号上吃的东西和受到的待遇远比他在皮戈瑞·波康比农场要好得多。有几天,他因为想念慈祥的老姨妈而有些烦恼(尤其是他晕船那个时候),但现在鲁滨逊变得非常的满足和快乐。他掌握了不晕船的本领,在甲板上蹦来跳去的,直到他变得太胖,再也懒得去动了。

Chapter Seven

It must not be supposed for one moment that Robinson was ill-treated on board ship. Quite the contrary. He was even better fed and more petted on the "Pound of Candles" than he had been at Piggery Porcombe. So, after a few days' fretting for his kind old aunts (especially while he was seasick), Robinson became perfectly contented and happy. He found what is called his "sea legs"; and he scampered about the deck until the time when he became too fat and lazy to scamper.

厨师不厌其烦地为他煮麦片粥。满满一麻袋的粗磨粉和一麻袋土豆看来就是专门为鲁滨逊准备的。他想吃多少就吃多少，吃饱了，就躺在暖和的甲板上，真是心满意足。当船驶入南方更暖和的地方，他变得越来越懒了。大副把他当做宠物，船员给他吃精美食品。厨师按摩他的背，在他身体两侧搔痒———但是他的肋骨部位感觉不到痒，因为储存了很厚的脂肪。只有那只黄公猫和船长巴纳巴斯·布彻不愿把他当做笑料。船长巴纳巴斯·布彻是个性格暴躁的人。

The cook was never tired of boiling porridge for him. A whole sack full of meal and a sack of potatoes appeared to have been provided especially for his benefit and pleasure. He could eat as much as he pleased. It pleased him to eat a great deal and to lie on the warm boards of the deck. He got lazier and lazier as the ship sailed south into warmer weather. The mate made a pet of him; the crew gave him tit-bits. The cook rubbed his back and scratched his sides — his ribs could not be tickled, because he had laid so much fat on. The only persons who refused to treat him as a joke were the yellow tom-cat and Captain Barnabas Butcher, who was of a sour disposition.

黄猫对鲁滨逊的态度是复杂的，显然他不赞成喂他玉米粉粥。他曾神秘地说过不恰当的贪婪以及过度放纵的后果，但他没有讲清可能会有哪些后果，因为黄猫自己既不喜欢黄色的食物也不喜欢精美事物。鲁滨逊认为这种提醒可能出自黄猫对他的成见，并非不友好，但听起来有些令人伤心，而且也似乎是不祥之兆。

这只猫在爱情上受到了挫折。他对人生悲观的态度，一部分是由于他和猫头鹰分手造成的。那只温柔的母鸟——一只来自莱普兰德的雪白猫头鹰，和去格林兰的一艘北方扑鲸船走了，而"坎德尔斯的庞德"号是驶向热带海洋的。

The attitude of the cat was perplexing to Robinson. Obviously it disapproved of the maize meal porridge business, and it spoke mysteriously about the impropriety of greediness, and about the disastrous results of over-indulgence. But it did not explain what those results might be, and as the cat itself cared neither for yellow meal nor'taties, Robinson thought that its warnings might arise from prejudice. It was not unfriendly. It was mournful and foreboding.

The cat itself was crossed in love. Its morose and gloomy outlook upon life was partly the result of separation from the owl. That sweet hen-bird, a snowy owl of Lapland, had sailed upon a northern whaler, bound for Greenland. Whereas the "Pound of Candles" was heading for the tropic seas.

因为这段爱情故事,猫没有心思工作,而且和厨师的关系非常糟糕。他没有替船长擦黑皮靴也没有替他洗衣服,反而日日夜夜待在帆索上,在月光下唱小夜曲。偶尔他来到甲板上,规劝鲁滨逊。

那只猫从来没有明确地告诉他为什么不应该多吃,但他常提到一个神秘的日子(鲁滨逊从来记不住)—— 船长布彻的生日,每年这一天,他都要准备一顿特别的晚餐来庆祝。

"这就是为什么他们在储存苹果的原因。那些洋葱已经不行了,因为热,发芽了。我听船长布彻告诉厨师,只要有苹果作调味汁,有没有洋葱无关紧要。"

Therefore the cat neglected its duties, and was upon the worst of terms with the cook. Instead of blacking boots and valeting the Captain, it spent days and nights in the rigging, serenading the moon. Between times it came down on deck, and remonstrated with Robinson.

It never told him plainly why he ought not to eat so much; but it referred frequently to a mysterious date (which Robinson could never remember) — the date of Captain Butcher's birthday, which he celebrated annually by an extra good dinner.

"That's what they are saving up apples for. The onions are done — sprouted with the heat. I heard Captain Barnabas tell the cook that onions were of no consequence as long as there were apples for sauce."

鲁滨逊没有太用心听，事实上，他和猫都在观望船下面游动的银色鱼群。因为没有风，船停止前进了。厨师穿过甲板溜达过来，看猫在看什么。他见到这么多鲜活的鱼，喜出望外地叫了起来。不一会儿，一半的船员都来钓鱼了，他们用一点红毛线和少量的饼干作鱼饵。水手长用闪亮的扣子作鱼饵，捕到很多鱼。

用扣子钓鱼，最大的缺点就是鱼在被拉上甲板的过程中，很多都掉回到海里去了。最后船长布彻允许船员把小工作艇降到水面。五位水手上了小艇，猫也跳了下去。他们一钓就是好几个小时，海

Robinson paid no attention. In fact, he and the cat were both on the side of the ship, watching a shoal of silvery fishes. The ship was completely becalmed. The cook strolled across the deck to see what the cat was looking at and exclaimed joyfully at sight of fresh fish. Presently half the crew were fishing. They baited their lines with bits of scarlet wool and bits of biscuit; and the boatswain had a successful catch on a line baited with a shiny button.

The worst of button fishing was that so many fish dropped off while being hauled on deck. Consequently Captain Butcher allowed the crew to launch the jolly boat, which was let down from some iron contraption called "the davits" on to the glassy surface of the sea. Five sailors got into the boat; the cat jumped

上没有一丝风。

　　猫不在的时候,鲁滨逊安稳地在温暖的甲板上睡着了。后来,

in also. They fished for hours. There was not a breath of wind.
　　In the absence of the cat, Robinson fell asleep peacefully upon the warm deck. Later he was disturbed by the voices of

他被大副和厨师的说话声吵醒了,他们没有去钓鱼。大副说:

"我可不喜欢吃中暑的猪里脊。厨师,把他弄醒,要不扔块帆布把他盖上。我自己是在农场长大的,猪绝不能睡在炎热的太阳下。"

"那是为什么?"厨师问道。

"会中暑的,"大副回答道,"而且,会把皮肤灼伤脱皮,也会破坏烤猪脆皮的外观。"

就在这个时候,一块又厚又脏的粗帆布扔下来,盖在鲁滨逊的身上。鲁滨逊在下面又挣扎又踢打,并发出急促的"咕噜"声。

the mate and the cook, who had not gone fishing. The former was saying:

"I don't fancy loin of pork with sunstroke, Cooky. Stir him up; or else throw a piece of sail cloth over him. I was bred on a farm myself. Pigs should never be let sleep in a hot sun."

"As why?"inquired the cook.

"Sunstroke,"replied the mate. "Likewise it scorches the skin; makes it peely like; spoils the look of the crackling."

At this point a rather heavy dirty piece of sail cloth was flung over Robinson, who struggled and kicked with sudden grunts.

"大副,他听见你说什么了吗?"厨师低声地问道。

"不知道,无所谓,反正他下不了船。"大副回答道,并且点起了烟斗。

"这可能会影响他的胃口,他本来吃得很好。"厨师说。

不一会儿,传来了船长巴纳巴斯·布彻的说话声,在船舱里午休之后,他来到了甲板上。

"到桅杆上去,根据经纬度,用望远镜观察一下地平线。根据海图和罗盘,我们应该在群岛之中了。"船长布彻说。

"Did he hear you, Matey?" asked the cook in a lower voice.

"Don't know; don't matter; he can't get off the ship," replied the mate, lighting his pipe.

"Might upset his appetite; he's feeding beautiful," said the cook.

Presently the voice of Captain Barnabas Butcher was heard. He had come up on deck after a siesta below in his cabin.

"Proceed to the crow's nest on the main mast; observe the horizon through a telescope according to latitude and longitude. We ought to be amongst the archipelago by the chart and compass," said the voice of Captain Butcher.

船长低沉而果断的声音通过帆布传到了鲁滨逊的耳中,可是大副没有听从命令,当没有别人在旁边听的时候,他偶尔会与船长争执。

"我的鸡眼很疼。"大副说。

"派那只猫上去。"船长布彻简洁地命令道。

"猫到下面小艇上钓鱼去了。"

"那么去找他。"船长布彻发脾气了,"他已经两周没有给我的靴子上鞋油了。"船长下去了,也就是说由梯子下到船舱,在舱里他

It reached the ears of Robinson through the sail cloth in muffled tones, but peremptory; although it was not so received by the mate, who occasionally contradicted the Captain when no one else was listening.

"My corns are very painful," said the mate.

"Send the cat up," ordered Captain Barnabas briefly.

"The cat is out in the boat fishing."

"Fetch him in then," said Captain Barnabas, losing his temper. "He has not blacked my boots for a fortnight." He went below; that is, down a step-ladder into his cabin, where he proceeded to work out the latitude and longitude again, in

又开始继续计算纬度和经度,搜寻群岛所在的方位。

"希望在下星期四以前他的脾气会改一点,否则他就吃不到烤猪肉!"大副对厨师说。

他们溜达到甲板的另一头,去看捕到了什么鱼,小艇马上就该回来了。

由于风平浪静,小艇就留在镜子一样的海面上过夜,被拴在了"坎德尔斯的庞德"号船尾的一个舷窗(或称为船窗)下面。

猫带着望远镜被派到桅杆上。他在上面待了一会儿就下来了,

search of the archipelago.

"It's to be hoped that he mends his temper before next Thursday, or he won't enjoy roast pork!" said the mate to the cook.

They strolled to the other end of the deck to see what fish had been caught; the boat was coming back.

As the weather was perfectly calm, it was left over night upon the glassy sea, tied below a port-hole (or ship's window) at the stern of the "Pound of Candles".

The cat was sent up the mast with a telescope; it remained

小猪鲁滨逊的故事
The Tale of Little Pig Robinson

并且报告说什么也没看到,这是非常不真实的。那天晚上,"坎德尔斯的庞德"号船没有特别的守望或警戒,因为海面上十分平静,而猫本来是应该在那里监视的。船上其余的成员都在打牌。

　　猫或鲁滨逊都没有这样做。猫注意到帆布下面有轻微的动静,他发现鲁滨逊吓得全身发抖,泪水像小河一样流下来,因为他无意中听到了关于猪肉的谈话。

there for some time. When it came down it reported quite untruthfully that there was nothing in sight. No particular watch or look-out was kept that night upon the "Pound of Candles" because the ocean was so calm. The cat was supposed to watch — if anybody did. All the rest of the ship's company played cards.

　　Not so the cat or Robinson. The cat had noticed a slight movement under the sail cloth. It found Robinson shivering with fright and in floods of tears. He had overheard the conversation about pork.

"我肯定已经给你足够的暗示了。"猫对鲁滨逊说,"你认为他们这样喂养你是为了什么?现在你别再扯着嗓子噢噢叫了,你这个小傻瓜!如果你能听我的,不哭了,事情就好办了,就像吸鼻烟那样容易。你多少还能划点船(鲁滨逊偶尔出去划过船,还抓到几只螃蟹)。其实,你不需要走得太远。我在桅杆上可以看到 N.N.E. 岛上的蓬树顶梢,群岛海峡对'坎德尔斯的庞德'号来说太浅了,我会躲避其他船只。跟我来,照着我说的去做!"那只猫说。

那只猫,一方面出于无私的友谊,另一方面由于对厨师和船长

"I'm sure I have given you enough hints," said the cat to Robinson. "What do you suppose they were feeding you up for? Now don't start squealing, you little fool! It's as easy as snuff, if you will listen and stop crying. You can row, after a fashion." (Robinson had been out fishing occasionally and caught several crabs.) "Well, you have not far to go; I could see the top of the Bong tree on an island N.N.E., when I was up the mast. The straits of the archipelago are too shallow for the "Pound of Candles", and I'll scuttle all the other boats. Come along, and do what I tell you!" said the cat.

The cat, actuated partly by unselfish friendship, and partly by a grudge against the cook and Captain Barnabas Butcher,

巴纳巴斯·布彻怀恨在心,他帮助鲁滨逊寻找各种各样的必需品:鞋子、火漆、小刀、扶手椅、鱼具、草帽、锯子、粘蝇纸、煮土豆的锅、望远镜、水壶、罗盘、斧子、一桶面粉、一桶粗磨粉、一小桶淡水、平底玻璃杯、茶壶、钉子、水桶、螺丝刀——

"我想起来了,"猫说,"要做的就是拿着手钻,绕过甲板,把还在'坎德尔斯的庞德'号上的三只小船钻三个大洞。"

这时候,下面开始传来了不妙的声音,那些玩牌手气不好的海员开始厌烦打牌了。于是,猫急忙与鲁滨逊告别,把他推向船的一侧,他就顺着粗绳滑进下面的小船里。猫解开了绳子的上端,接着

assisted Robinson to collect a varied assortment of necessaries. Shoes, sealing-wax, a knife, an armchair, fishing tackle, a straw hat, a saw, fly papers, a potato pot, a telescope, a kettle, a compass, a hammer, a barrel of flour, another of meal, a keg of fresh water, a tumbler, a teapot, nails, a bucket, a screwdriver —

"That reminds me," said the cat, and what did it do but go round the deck with a gimlet and bore large holes in the three boats that remained on board the "Pound of Candles".

By this time there began to be ominous sounds below; those of the sailors who had had bad hands were beginning to be tired of carding. So the cat took a hasty farewell of Robinson, pushed him over the ship's side, and he slid down the rope

小猪鲁滨逊的故事
The Tale of Little Pig Robinson

把绳子扔了下去,然后爬到帆索上,装作在监视时睡着了。

鲁滨逊跌撞了几下,坐到划桨的位子上,他的腿显然有点太短了。在船舱里,船长布彻把牌停下来。他手里拿着一张牌,静听着(厨师趁机偷看了下面的牌),然后继续把牌甩下去,甩牌的声音盖过了平静海面上的划桨声。

又打了几圈牌之后,两个海员离开船舱,上了甲板。他们看见远处有一个又大又黑的甲虫似的东西。一个人说,这是一只巨大的蟑螂,用后腿游泳。另一个人说那是海豚,他们大声争论起来。在

into the boat. The cat unfastened the upper end of the rope and threw it after him. Then it ascended the rigging and pretended to sleep upon its watch.

Robinson stumbled somewhat in taking his seat at the oars. His legs were short for rowing. Captain Barnabas in the cabin suspended his deal, a card in his hand, listening (the cook took the opportunity to look under the card), then he went on slapping down the cards, which drowned the sound of oars upon the placid sea.

After another hand, two sailors left the cabin and went on deck. They noticed something having the appearance of a large black beetle in the distance. One of them said it was an enormous cockroach, swimming with its hind legs. The other said it was a dolphinium. They disputed, rather loudly.

厨师发牌以后，船长布彻打了一局无主牌的牌 ——船长布彻登上甲板，说道：

"把望远镜给我拿来。"

望远镜不见了，他的鞋、火漆、罗盘、煮土豆的锅、草帽、斧子、钉子、水桶、螺丝刀和扶手椅全不见了。

船长布彻命令道："乘工作艇去看看那是什么东西。"

"一切都挺好的，也许那是海豚呢？"大副表示反对。

"哎呀，我的天呀，工作艇不见了！"一个水手大声地说。

Captain Barnabas, who had had a hand with no trumps at all after the cook dealing — Captain Barnabas came on deck and said:

"Bring me my telescope."

The telescope had disappeared; likewise the shoes, the sealing-wax, the compass, the potato pot, the straw hat, the hammer, the nails, the bucket, the screwdriver, and the armchair.

"Take the jolly boat and see what it is," ordered Captain Butcher.

"All jolly fine, but suppose it is a dolphinium?" said the mate mutinously.

"Why, bless my life, the jolly boat is gone!" exclaimed a sailor.

"用另一只船,把三只船全用上。这是猪和猫干的!"船长咆哮道。

"不是,长官,猫在帆索上睡着了。"

"真讨厌,那只猫!把那头猪弄回来!否则,那苹果汁就浪费了!"厨师尖叫着,跳来跳去,舞着刀和叉。

吊艇架移开,船放下了,水面上溅起一片片水花。所有水手都跌跌撞撞地上了船,开始疯狂地划船。但他们又拼命地划回到"坎德尔斯的庞德"号,因为每只船都漏得很厉害,这都要归功于猫出的主意。

"Take another boat, take all the three other boats; it's that pig and that cat!" roared the Captain.

"Nay, sir, the cat's up the rigging asleep."

"Bother the cat! Get the pig back! The apple sauce will be wasted!" shrieked the cook, dancing about and brandishing a knife and fork.

The davits were swung out, the boats were let down with a swish and a splash, all the sailors tumbled in, and rowed frantically. And most of them were glad to row frantically back to the "Pound of Candles". For every boat leaked badly, thanks to the cat.

第八章

鲁滨逊乘小艇逃离了"坎德尔斯的庞德"号,他紧紧地拽住双桨,桨对他来说实在太重了。太阳落山了,但是据我所知,在热带 —— 我从来没有去过 —— 海面有一种磷光闪烁。当鲁滨逊抬起他的桨,闪烁的水珠就像金刚钻似的从桨叶上一粒一粒地掉下来。不一会儿,月亮开始从地平线上升起 —— 好像半个巨大的银盘在夜空中升起来。

Chapter Eight

Robinson rowed away from the "Pound of Candles". He tugged steadily at the oars. They were heavy for him. The sun had set, but I understand that in the tropics — I have never been there — there is a phosphorescent light upon the sea. When Robinson lifted his oars, the sparkling water dripped from the blades like diamonds. And presently the moon began to rise above the horizon — rising like half a great silver plate.

鲁滨逊倚靠在桨上休息，凝视着那艘大船。在月光下，小船荡漾在宁静的海面上。在这个时候——他已距大船四分之一英里之遥——两个海员登上甲板，以为他的小船是一只游泳的甲虫。

Robinson rested on his oars and gazed at the ship, motionless in the moonlight, on a sea without a ripple. It was at this moment — he being a quarter of a mile away — that the two sailors came on deck, and thought his boat was a swimming beetle.

"坎德尔斯的庞德"号已经看不见了,船上的喧嚣也听不到了,但鲁滨逊很快就察觉到三只小船正在追赶他,他情不自禁地尖叫起来,开始拼命划船。在他还没有累得筋疲力尽的时候,三只小船调头回去了。这时鲁滨逊才想起猫用手钻干的活儿,知道那几只船全漏了。在晚上剩下的时间里,他不慌不忙、静静地划着船。他还没有睡意,空气非常舒适凉爽。第二天,天气很热,但鲁滨逊在帆布下睡得很熟。猫考虑得很周到,让他带上了那张帆布,以便用它来支帐篷。

Robinson was too far away to see or hear the uproar on board the "Pound of Candles"; but he did presently perceive that three boats were starting in pursuit. Involuntarily he commenced to squeal, and rowed frantically. But before he had time to exhaust himself by racing, the ship's boats turned back. Then Robinson remembered the cat's work with the gimlet, and he knew that the boats were leaking. For the rest of the night he rowed quietly, without haste. He was not inclined to sleep, and the air was pleasantly cool. Next day it was hot, but Robinson slept soundly under the sail cloth, which the cat had been careful to send with him, in case he wished to rig up a tent.

小猪鲁滨逊的故事
The Tale of Little Pig Robinson

大船消失在海的尽头 —— 要知道，大海并不是完全水平的，鲁滨逊先是看不见船身了，然后又看不见甲板和部分桅杆了，最后什么也看不见了。

鲁滨逊原来是依靠那只船来导航的，现在失去了方向的标志，于是他转过身来看他的罗盘 —— 这时，船颠簸了两下，碰到了沙滩，幸好船没有搁浅。

鲁滨逊从船上站起来，用桨往后划。他环顾四周，只能看到蓬树的顶梢！

The ship receded from view — you know the sea is not really flat. First he could not see the hull, then he could not see the deck, then only part of the masts, then nothing at all.

Robinson had been steering his course by the ship. Having lost sight of this direction sign, he turned round to consult his compass — when bump, bump, the boat touched a sandbank. Fortunately it did not stick.

Robinson stood up in the boat, working one oar backwards, and gazing around. What should he see but the top of the Bong tree!

连续划了半小时以后,他来到一座又广阔又肥沃的岛屿的沙滩上,他按照最可靠的方法,在合适的隐蔽的海湾靠了岸。那里有一股滚烫的溪水流淌到银色的海滩上,岸边到处都是牡蛎。树上长满

Half an hour's rowing brought him to the beach of a large and fertile island. He landed in the most approved manner in a convenient sheltered bay, where a stream of boiling water flowed down the silvery strand. The shore was covered with

了圆形小糖果,就叫它甘薯吧,相当于一种红薯,吃起来好像都是烤好了的。面包果树结了冰糕和松饼,它们都已经被晒熟了。这样,鲁滨逊再也不必为麦片粥而叹息了。蓬树在头顶上高高耸起。

如果你想知道有关这个岛的更详细的情况,你必须读一读《鲁滨逊漂流记》。蓬树岛很像《鲁滨逊漂流记》里的那个岛,惟独没有那个岛上的缺点。我从来没有去过那儿,因此我完全靠那只猫头鹰和那只猫咪的报告,他们是一年半以后去的,在那里度过了愉快的蜜月。他们热情洋溢地谈到那里的气候 ——只是对猫头鹰来说有一点太热了。

oysters. Acid drops and sweets grew upon the trees. Yams, which are a sort of sweet potato, abounded ready cooked. The bread-fruit tree grew iced cakes and muffins, ready baked; so no pig need sigh for porridge. Overhead towered the Bong tree.

If you want a more detailed description of the island, you must read "Robinson Crusoe". The island of the Bong tree was very like Crusoe's, only without its drawbacks. I have never been there myself, so I rely upon the report of the Owl and the Pussy Cat, who visited it eighteen months later, and spent a delightful honeymoon there. They spoke enthusiastically about the climate — only it was a little too warm for the Owl.

后来，斯达姆比和小狗蒂普金斯拜访了鲁滨逊，发现他非常满足，而且身体也棒极了，他一点也不想回到斯蒂茅斯了。据我所知，他可能还会在那个岛住下去。他长得越来越胖，但船上的厨师再也找不到他了。

（完）

Later on Robinson was visited by Stumpy and little dog Tipkins. They found him perfectly contented, and in the best of good health. He was not at all inclined to return to Stymouth. For anything I know he may be living there still upon the island. He grew fatter and fatter and more fatterer; and the ship's cook never found him.

THE END